BELIEVERS BIBLE STUDY SERIES

the miracles *of* JESUS

STUDY GUIDE AND NOTES

KEN WILLIAMS

WestBow Press books may be ordered through booksellers or by contacting:

WestBow Press
A Division of Thomas Nelson & Zondervan
1663 Liberty Drive
Bloomington, IN 47403
www.westbowpress.com
844-714-3454

Any quotations from the Bible are from the English Standard Version.

Cover design by Jessica Williams.
Cover photograph of wheat field by Jez Timms.

ISBN: 979-8-3850-1459-0 (sc)
ISBN: 979-8-3850-1460-6 (e)

Library of Congress Control Number: 2023924257

Print information available on the last page.

WestBow Press rev. date: 5/24/2024

To my wife Kathy, to my sons Chris and Sean, to my daughter-in-law Jessica, to my grandchildren Parker and Sybil, and to the men who have made up Believers Bible Study for over twenty years.

Additionally and most importantly, to the glory and majesty of God the Father, God the Son, and God the Holy Spirit. There is no life without the Trinity, and there is total life with the Three-in-One. Praise God from whom all blessings flow!

CONTENTS

PREFACE
The Beginnings of the Believers Bible Study Series

The Believers Bible Study Series was developed as a result of a Bible study that started over twenty years ago in Texas. At the time it began, I had really not given much thought to formalizing the individual lessons into a comprehensive series of studies. But as they say, God had another idea!

A friend and I knew some teenagers and their dads who wanted to know more about the Bible, so the friend and I started an informal study during the summer months because we all had a common interest in knowing more about God's Word. The first year we met only in the summer, and when the teenagers returned to their church youth group in the fall where they met once a week in study and prayer, my friend and I were right there to lead the group.

Eventually, however, the study refocused and became a time when the adults got together to enjoy fellowship with one another while learning what the Bible could and should mean to each of us. As time went by, the study adopted the formal name of Believers Bible Study, and it continues to meet weekly. For most of the years we have been together, we met in person, but more recently even with Covid restrictions, my relocation to Oregon, and most of the men in the study living in Texas, the study has stayed alive and continues to flourish due to the modern-day miracle of Zoom.

In the early days, there were some studies based on books by Christian authors, primarily by John MacArthur. However, for the past twelve to fifteen years, the study has used one text—the Bible. Although we still use commentaries and other reference sources to help with answers to the questions, the singular focus is on God's Word. After all, it is a *Bible* study! (Note: I have used, almost entirely, the *English Standard Version* [ESV] as it is a word-for-word translation rather than a thought-for-thought version, but there is no version required or recommended for the study.)

I have written the lessons the entire time the study has been in existence. I have chosen to do that for various reasons. First, by writing the lessons rather than depending on what someone else has written, I force myself to learn what the verses are saying to me. Second, I love to write, and I have written extensively for this study, for other studies, and for my professional career in human resources. Third and most importantly, I have wanted to create studies that will help others get as excited about the Bible as I am!

So I am greatly excited for the publication of this first study in the Believers Bible Study Series *The Miracles of Jesus.* It is the intention that more studies will follow, such as *The Parables of Jesus, Daniel, Hebrews, Men of the Old Testament,* the *Gospels,* the *Letters of Paul,* and the epistles. Stay tuned!

ACKNOWLEDGMENTS

There are numerous people to thank for their contribution to the Believers Bible Study Series *The Miracles of Jesus*, but there are certain ones who deserve to be recognized by name.

- Kathy Williams, my wife since 1966, who, without her encouragement, I would have dropped the project many times, and without her resolute editing the book would be harder to read and more difficult to understand.

- Martha Davis, a close personal friend of my wife Kathy, who voluntarily did further editing on the book picking up on nuances that had been formerly missed and giving me encouragement at just the right times.

- *Special note: Kathy and Martha spent innumerable hours on the phone, on Zoom calls, by email, and by text working through each and every part of the study. Without them, this study would have never been completed.*

- Chris Williams, one of my twin sons, who was constantly ready to assist with the formatting of the book with the expertise he developed as an intranet professional for an outdoor products company and a national restaurant chain.

- Jessica Williams, my daughter-in-law, Chris's wife, and a graphics design expert, who designed the cover, title page and logo, and gave invaluable formatting advice.

- Sean Williams, the other of my twin sons, who provided both encouragement and expertise in areas that were baffling to me.

- The men, the originals of the weekly time together known as Believers Bible Study, who met faithfully first in person and then on Zoom. Without these men, the study would have been less lively, less fulfilling, and less focused on God's Word.

- Above all, thanks goes to my Lord and Savior Jesus Christ who provided the material for the lessons. Without Him and His claiming me as His own, this book would have been an absolute impossibility.

INTRODUCTION

When I decided to develop the Believers Bible Study Series so that others could learn more about the Bible through study, one of the first decisions was the topic. Since I had previously led a study on the miracles of Jesus, it seemed logical to make the miracles the first study in the series. Besides having already led a study on this topic, there were three other reasons I chose to do so.

First, Jesus used many methods of teaching, but miracles along with parables and sermons were three of the main ways He taught. Therefore, it seemed appropriate that the first study I wrote would naturally deal with one of those three topics. If they were good enough for Jesus, they certainly should be good enough for me!

Second, the miracles touched the common people most significantly. That's not to say that others were not included in the miraculous work of Jesus, but it is to say that Jesus had great compassion for those who had little or no hope and those who were looked down on by society. People who were desperate on so many levels were the ones He chose to help most often.

Third, the apostle John had a unique perspective on the miracles because he saw each and every miracle as a spiritual sign of what Jesus was doing. If a person was blind and physically healed, it was a sign that his or her spiritual blindness was also cured. If a deaf person was physically healed, then the deaf person would be healed spiritually as well, a sign to truly hear and understand the truth of God's Word.

While there could be other reasons, I believe that miracles should take center stage in my first study for the Believers Bible Study Series. It is intended for other studies to follow with other topics, and they will all be important because they are all God's Holy Word.

WHAT DOES AN INDIVIDUAL STUDY LESSON LOOK LIKE?

There is a basic format for each of the lessons.

- Opening notes that speak to something related to the topic of the miracle in general, something in the previous lesson, something in the current lesson, or any combination.

- A series of questions—fifteen to twenty-five—that seek written responses. That is, there are no true/false or multiple-choice questions. The questions are open-ended in an attempt to lead participants to think about their answers.

- For the most part, questions are based on the scripture selection for the lesson or on related Bible verses.

- Additionally, there are questions that elicit answers from related quotes and information from books, articles, web pages, commentaries, and other sources.

- Some questions are labeled *Challenge*. These questions are somewhat more difficult and may require further reading or research in order to provide an answer. Commentaries and other extra-biblical resources may be used. If these questions prove too difficult to answer, the student may choose to omit answering them.

- Throughout the lessons, there are statements, quotes, and relevant thoughts designed to stimulate further thinking about a particular passage, topic, or idea.

- Additionally, other statements are designed for introspection or personal reflection. These may or may not have questions connected to them.

BONUS SECTION
LEADING OTHERS IN BIBLE STUDY

Included at the end of *The Miracles of Jesus* study is a bonus section on preparing to lead others in a group Bible study. It is free for anyone to use in a Bible study.

It provides in-depth information on how to lead others:

- Keys to an Effective Study,
- The Inductive Bible Study Method,
- Step-by-Step Recommendations,
- Guidelines for Managing a Group, and
- FAQs.

Using this bonus section will help you as you lead a group and enable you to encourage and guide them as you study God's Word together.

This bonus section *Leading Others in Bible Study* will be available in every study of the Believers Bible Study Series.

LESSON 1
Introduction to Miracles

Jesus used various methods of teaching in the Bible; the two most prominent are the *miracles* and the *parables.* Although there are other parts of the Bible that can be considered parables, there is little agreement on which of those are parables and which are not. Some might be better classified as *illustrations* or *allegories.* However, there is no real disagreement about miracles. Even in the Old Testament, before the time of Jesus, there are events that can clearly be classified as miracles, but this is primarily a New Testament study of most of the miracles Jesus performed while on earth.

John MacArthur, on his *Grace to You* website,[2] says the following about miracles, "What is a miracle? Let me give you a simple definition. A miracle is an interference with nature by a supernatural power. A miracle is something outside our box invading our little box, something outside our world coming into our world and making waves and ripples. Miracles are events in the external world wrought by the power of God. A miracle is God stepping into the universe, setting aside the normal laws of nature to do a supernatural act. And therein you have the definition of miracles, really. They were mighty works to create wonder, to act as a sign.

"And you know where miracles are supposed to point? Outside the box. Miracles are designed by God to invade the natural world, to show the natural world that there is a supernatural world. And if you continually try to explain miracles away by natural reasoning, what you are doing is just acting like an atheist. You're disallowing God."[1]

From a biblical standpoint, Acts 2:22 (New Living Translation) says, "People of Israel, listen! God publicly endorsed Jesus the Nazarene by doing powerful miracles, wonders, and signs through him, as you well know." While every word in the Bible is important, this verse is important because it uses three words that are central to understanding the miracles: power(ful), wonders, and signs.

Miracles are aligned with the word *power* because they show the mighty power of God which is manifested in Jesus because He is God incarnate. This word points to a new and higher force that is at work in the lower world that humans inhabit. Powers, the plural, is translated in various places in the Bible as wonderful works, mighty works, and miracles.

The word *wonders* is representative of the state of mind that is manifested in an individual when he or she witnesses a miracle. Jesus performing a miracle is a display of power that is contrary to what previous expectations could have produced. Because of this, attention must be given to their purpose and to their inner spiritual appeal.

Finally, *signs* is an important term to understand because

---

[1] John MacArthur, "The Bible Verifiable by Miracles" (November 3, 1974), accessed March 1, 2019, https://www.gty.org/library/sermons-library/1346/the-bible-verifiable-by-miracles.

it carries the significance of miracles as being seals by which God authenticated the miracle worker himself. With this word Christians know that the miracle is an indication of the presence and working of God. It is proof of the genuineness of revelation and proof or evidence furnished by one set of facts to the reality and genuineness of another. (John in his writings refers to all the miracles as signs because they point to what the Old Testament tells us Jesus was to be.)

Regarding a specific book in the New Testament, the book of Mark is a Gospel that is particularly important to the study of Jesus's miracles. Why is that? Warren Wiersbe in *The Bible Exposition Commentary* explains this importance:

> Mark, the first of the four Gospels to be written, has often been called the "action Gospel" because of its emphasis on Jesus' deeds rather than his teaching. This is also true regarding Jesus' miracles, for Mark contains more miracles proportionately than any of the other Gospels. R. H. Fuller in his *Interpreting the Miracles* has noted five groups in Mark. The first centers on Jesus' authority over demons (1:21–39). The second concerns Jesus' authority over the Law and conflict with his opponents (1:40–3:6). These result in fame but occasion his refusal to allow his true identity as Son of God to be known. The third group (3:7–30) contains exorcisms and the Beelzebub controversy, centering on his power over Satan. The fourth group (4:35–5:43) contains especially powerful miracles (stilling the storm, the Gadarene demoniac, the raising of Jairus' daughter)

> and center on the disciples, as Jesus thereby reveals to them the meaning of the kingdom and seeks to overcome their own spiritual dullness. The fifth and final group (6:30–8:26) continues the theme of the disciples' misunderstanding and prepares the way for the passion, with the message regarding the bread, blindness, and the judgment of God.[2]

Also, in his "Miracles in Mark," Wiersbe talks about miracles performed by five different entities: (1) those performed directly by God, (2) those performed directly by Jesus, (3) those performed by the Holy Spirit, (4) those performed by servants of God, and (5) those performed by evil agents.

There are a couple of important points to note about Jesus regarding the miracles He performed. First, He never used His power of performing miracles for His own safety and aggrandizement. Second, He never worked a single miracle on His own behalf. He enriched others by choosing to remain impoverished. This may be one of the more fascinating aspects of the miracles of Jesus because His human side might have wanted some of the glory for what He did. However, as He told His followers, He came to do what His followers are expected to do—serve others, and it is difficult to have a true servant's heart if someone is looking for glory for themselves.

---

[2] Warren W. Wiersbe, "Miracles in Mark," in *The Bible Exposition Commentary, Bible Exposition Commentary,* (Electronic Edition. Wheaton: Victor Books, a Division of Scripture Press Publications, Inc., 1996), https://www.logos.com.

STUDY GUIDE

Miracle. A surprising and welcome event that is not explicable by natural or scientific laws and is therefore considered to be the work of a divine agency. A highly improbable or extraordinary event, development, or accomplishment that brings very welcome consequences. An amazing product or achievement, or an outstanding example of something.[3]

Opening Questions

1. Is there anything from the introduction to the miracles that impressed you? If so, what was it, and why did it impress you?

2. Does the secular definition of a miracle in the quote above miss the mark from a Christian point of view? If so, how?

3. Think about miracles in the Old Testament that may be familiar to you. After reflecting on them for a few minutes, select one or more and explain why the miracle is (or miracles are) particularly important to you.

4. Now consider the whole Bible, both testaments, and select what you see as the most prominent and important miracle in the Bible. Explain your choice.

---

[3] "Miracle," accessed March 1, 2019, https://languages.oup.com.

General Questions about Biblical Miracles

Miracles in the Old Testament: To the Hebrew, a miracle was nothing more or less than an act of God. A miracle was signified by its revelatory significance and/or its connection with crucial points in the history of God's people—the exodus, the conquest of the Jordan, and the battle against the insidious Baal worship of the prophetic period. The miracles of Genesis—striking blind the inhabitants of Sodom, the flood, and Babel—all signify the wrath of God upon those who have turned against him. This is the other side of redemptive history—the judgment of God upon those who are not his people.[4]

5. The miracles in the Exodus account have two main focal points: (a) the absolute power of Yahweh over man-made gods and (b) the care and protection of God's people. From the Exodus account, give examples representing each of the focal points.

6. Miracles were infrequent in the writing of the prophets with two major exceptions. See what you can find out about miracles concerning the following:

    a. Jonah
    b. Daniel

7. One of the more mysterious miracles in the Bible is in the book of Hezekiah. What miraculous event occurs to Hezekiah, and what makes that miracle so mysterious?

---

[4] Walter A. Elwell, "Miracles in the Old Testament," in *Baker's Evangelical Dictionary of Biblical Theology* (Grand Rapids: Baker Book House Company, 1966).

8. If the miracles of the Old Testament signify the presence of God, what do the miracles of the New Testament signify? Read Luke 4:18–21. Then either quote directly from Luke or use your own words to summarize these verses.

9. Referring to the opening thoughts for this lesson, give an example of a miracle performed by each of the following:

    a. God directly
    b. Christ directly
    c. the Holy Spirit
    d. servants of God
    e. evil agents

Questions about One of Jesus's Miracles

God's Word Speaks

And there was a woman who had had a discharge of blood for twelve years, and who had suffered much under many physicians, and had spent all that she had, and was no better but rather grew worse. She had heard the reports about Jesus and came up behind him in the crowd and touched his garment. For she said, "If I touch even his garments, I will be made well." And immediately the flow of blood dried up, and she felt in her body that she was healed of her disease. And Jesus, perceiving in himself that power had gone out from him, immediately turned about in the crowd and said, "Who touched my garments?" And his disciples said to him, "You see the crowd pressing around you, and yet you say, 'Who touched me?'" And he looked around to see who had done it. But the woman, knowing what had happened to her, came in fear and trembling, and fell down before him and told him the whole truth. And he said to her, "Daughter, your faith has made you well; go in peace and be healed of your disease." (Mark 5:25–34)

10. When a miracle was performed in the Bible, there were, in many instances, no less than three persons or groups of people that would have been affected: (a) the one who performed the miracle, (b) the one on whom the miracle was performed, and (c) those who witnessed the miracle. With that in mind, consider the miracle of the woman who touched Jesus's garment and was cured of her bleeding illness. How did this miracle affect the following:

    a. the one who performed the miracle
    b. the one on whom the miracle was performed
    c. those who witnessed the miracle

11. What is the spiritual sign to which this miracle points?

12. Does verse 30 indicate Jesus lost some of His power? Explain whether you think it does or does not.

13. Other than the fact that Jesus chose to heal the woman, what was the sole reason that she was healed by the Lord?

14. What does this miracle say about Jesus, the woman, and the disciples?

Summary Questions

No phenomenon in nature, however unusual, no event in the course of God's providence, however unexpected, is a miracle unless it can be traced to the agency of man (including prayer under the term agency), and unless it is put forth as a proof of divine mission.[5]

15. Look at the quote above and explain what the author was saying when he used these words, "Unless it can be traced to the agency of man." What does that phrase mean to you? And who or what was the agency of man in the following miracles:

    a. ten plagues in Egypt (Exodus 7–12)
    b. Samson tearing down the pillars of the Philistines' temple (Judges 16:23–30)
    c. descent of the Holy Spirit on the listeners at the first Christian Pentecost (Acts 2:1–41)
    d. Peter raising Dorcas from the dead (Acts 9:36–42)

16. In your opinion, do miracles occur today? If so, give examples including the *agency of man.*

A major difference between magic and miracles is that magic draws upon power that is not directly from God, and miracles are the result of God's power intervening in the world. Magic is an attempt to circumvent God in the acquisition of knowledge or power. Another difference between magic and miracles is that magic does not glorify God, but miracles do. Another difference between magic and miracles is that magic involves manipulation and opposition to the truth, but miracles reveal the truth. Miracles and magic sometimes look the same, but their goals are different. Magic and illusion distract the eye from reality, while miracles draw the eye to reality. Miracles reveal; magic hides. Miracles are

[5] William Smith, *Smith's Bible Dictionary,* (Nashville: Thomas Nelson, 1986), digital-Logos Research Edition, logos release date 2001, https://www.logos.com.

an expression of creative power; magic uses what already exists. Miracles are a gift; magic is a studied skill. Miracles do not glorify men; magic seeks to be noticed and bring glory to the magician. Jesus was not a magician. He was the Son of God, known for His many miracles (John 7:31). Jesus told His enemies, "Do not believe me unless I do the works of my Father. But if I do them, even though you do not believe me, believe the works, that you may know and understand that the Father is in me, and I in the Father" (John 10:37–38). Jesus's miracles (or "signs" as John called them) are proof of who He is.[6]

[6] "What is the difference between miracles and magic?," accessed March 1, 2019, https://www.gotquestions.org/difference-miracles-magic.html.

LESSON 2

Jesus Turns Water into Wine at a Wedding

Miracles can be looked at in many different ways, and each of those ways may point to a new or different understanding of how God worked in the lives of people in the Old Testament and how Jesus Christ worked in the lives of people in the New Testament. When the miracles are looked at in terms of God's gifts given to man, they often have to do with *water.* Many miracles in the Bible have water as the primary focal point. A meaningful list of these *water* miracles requires some thinking and some research.

Unless you count the creation of the seas and rain as a miracle and unless you look at Noah building the ark so his family could be saved from the water as a miracle, you might start your list with any number of prominent, well-known miracles and go from there. Consider the following miracles that all have water as the focal point:

- the parting of the Red Sea,
- the waters of Marah during the Hebrews' wandering in the wilderness,
- the waters of Meribah during the Hebrews' wandering in the wilderness,

- the waters of Rephidin during the Hebrews' wandering in the wilderness,
- the parting of the Jordan River,
- the purifying of the waters of Jericho,
- the iron that floated,
- Elijah and the water at Mount Carmel,
- Jesus changing water to wine,
- Jesus stilling the wind and waters,
- Jesus walking on the sea, and
- the healing at the Bethesda pool.

There are others that have water as their focus, but those listed above are certainly an ample number to help get an idea of how often water plays a part in miracles in the Bible. However, just compiling a list is just that—a list, and it does not really tell much about why water is used so often. For that, one needs to get a better understanding of why water might have been a part of so many occurrences. Look at some of the ways the website biblestudytools.com talks about this important topic.

The word "water" is used in a variety of metaphorical ways in Scripture. It is used to symbolize troublesome times *(especially in many Psalms)*, enemies who attack and need to be overcome *(Psalms and prophets)*. In both the Old and New Testaments, the word is used for salvation and eternal life, which God offers humankind through faith in his Son *(Isaiah and Revelation)*. In John 4:10–15, part of Jesus' discourse with the Samaritan woman at the well, he speaks metaphorically of his salvation as "living water" and as "a spring of water welling up to eternal life."

Following along this same theme, water sometimes symbolizes the spiritual cleansing that comes with the acceptance of God's offer of salvation. In an important passage, Jesus identifies the "streams of living water" that flow from within those who believe in him with the Holy Spirit *(John 7:37–39).* Two times in Jeremiah, Yahweh is metaphorically identified as "the spring of living water" *(Jeremiah 2:13, 17:13* [italics mine]).

The reference to "water" in John 3:5 has been interpreted in various ways ... as in water baptism, a symbol of the Holy Spirit, and birth by water to be natural birth and birth by the Spirit to be the supernatural birth of being "born again" or regenerated.[7]

STUDY GUIDE

As the study of the miracle of changing water into wine begins, it might initially be seen as being frivolous and insignificant compared to many of Jesus's other miracles. However, this first of Jesus's miracles has a very deep meaning that will come to light as the study looks deeper into what Jesus did and why He did it.

Opening Questions

1. Just as in the introductory lesson, what did you find interesting, unusual, or intriguing in the introduction to this lesson?

2. *Tabletalk Magazine* states, "The miracles of Jesus are not so much supernatural violations of 'natural order' as they are supernatural restorations to nature ordered rightly, a picture of the way things ought to be."[8] How might you state that in a different way?

---

[7] "Water," https://www.biblestudytools.com/dictionary/water/.

[8] Doug Ponder, "Why Did Jesus Turn Water into Wine?," *Tabletalk Magazine* (December 2018), Ligonier Ministries.

Questions Leading Up to the Performance of the Miracle

According to the Mishnah, the wedding would take place on a Wednesday if the bride was a virgin and, on a Thursday, if she was a widow. The bridegroom and his friends made their way in procession to the bride's house. This was often done at night when there could be a spectacular torchlight procession. There were doubtless speeches and expressions of goodwill before the bride and groom went in procession to the groom's house, where the wedding banquet was held. It is probable that there was a religious ceremony, but we have no details. The processions and the feast are the principal items of which we have knowledge. The feast was prolonged and might last as long as a week.[9]

3. To provide a historical perspective, use the following verses to get an idea of what had taken place leading up to the time of this first miracle.

    a. Mark 1:9–11
    b. Mark 1:12–13 (There are more details on this in Luke 4.)
    c. John 1:19–34 (This is a longer text; share what you think is the most important event.)
    d. John 1:35–51

4. Why do you think this miracle was recorded only in the Gospel of John?

---

[9] "The First Sign: Jesus Turns Water into Wine (John 2:1–11)," accessed March 1, 2019, https://www.bible.org/seriespage/5-first-sign-jesus-turns-water-wine-john-21-11.

5. John 2 begins with "On the third day there was a wedding in Cana."

6. To what does the *third day* refer?

7. Where was Cana in relation to Jesus's hometown of Nazareth?

Questions about the Miracle

John 2:1–11

8. Since this is the first miracle of Jesus, one can assume He has not yet done anything extraordinary in the midst of his family or other people. Therefore, why do you think His mother Mary turns to Jesus and says, "They have no wine"? What is she hoping for or expecting at this point in Jesus's life?

9. Do you think Jesus's statement to His mother, "Woman, what does this have to do with me? My hour has not yet come," is disrespectful? Why or why not? Pay particular attention to the fact that He addresses her as "Woman."

10. With regard to Jesus's response to His mother, one commentary says, "(His response) simply serves to set the record straight by redefining His relationship to Mary, His earthly mother."[10] What do you think the commentator meant by that?

[10] "The First Sign: Jesus Turns Water into Wine (John 2:1–11)," https://www.bible.org/seriespage/5-first-sign-jesus-turns-water-wine-john-21-11.

11. Jesus makes a peculiar statement when He says, "My hour has not yet come." What does He mean by that? There certainly may be more than one thought regarding its meaning.

12. Mary then says to the servants, "Do whatever He tells you." What do you think her attitude was like when she made this statement? Was she offended, compliant, irritated, frustrated, or confused?

13. Read John 2:6–10 and outline the events that occur—what Jesus instructs, what the servants do, and the reactions to what happens. (Twelve events are identified, but there may be more or less depending on what you count as an event.)

14. See what you can find out about the containers that held the water at the feast. If you can, find data on how many containers there may have been, how much each container may have held, and what the purpose of the water is.

15. Since John calls this a sign rather than a miracle—as he does throughout his book regarding miracles—what is this particular miracle a sign of? There are numerous signs that can be identified.

16. What important statement does Jesus make by attending the wedding feast where the miracle occurred?

17. What is different about this miracle that sets it apart from most other miracles of Jesus?

18. How does this miracle affect the following:

    a. the one who performed the miracle
    b. the one for whom the miracle was performed
    c. the disciples who witnessed the miracle
    d. the servants who witnessed the miracle
    e. other people at the wedding feast (invited guests) who witnessed the miracle

Summary Questions

19. What spiritual message can be understood better by knowing that God turns water into the best wine rather than just an ordinary wine?

To begin with, the word John used in his book is not dunamis, which emphasizes power, but semeion, which means "a sign." What is a sign? Something that points beyond itself to something greater. It was not enough for people to believe in Jesus's works; they had to believe in Him and in the Father who sent Him (John 5:14–24). This explains why Jesus often added a sermon to the miracle and in that sermon interpreted the sign. In John 5, the healing of the paralytic on the Sabbath opened the way for a message on His deity, "the Lord of the Sabbath." The feeding of the 5,000 (John 6) led naturally into a sermon on the Bread of Life.[11]

[11] Wiersbe, "Jesus the Host," https://www.logos.com.

LESSON 3
Jesus Heals an Official's Son

Everyone knows what it is like to not be respected by those who are the closest. It might be with people with whom one works, customers with whom one does business, fellow church members, or even one's own family. It hurts deeply to be rejected, and it hurts even more when one is hurt by those who are believed to be loved ones. Biblically, there are some good examples of just this type of situation in the lives of God's servants.

Moses. Even though Moses was raised in the palace of the Egyptian pharaoh and was in fact raised as an Egyptian, somewhere deep down he knew that he was one of the Hebrew children. Because he felt that way, he killed an Egyptian guard who was mistreating one of his Hebrew brothers, but the next day when he was trying to resolve an argument between two Hebrew slaves, one of the slaves asked Moses if he planned to kill him as well. Moses thought he was going to be the hero of the nation, but instead, his own people rose up against him and caused him to flee into exile where he would remain for forty years.

Jacob. Jacob brought a lot of misery to himself (with his mother's help), but there were times when others brought misery upon him as well. When he fled his homeland, Jacob went to the land where Laban lived, a man who had two daughters—Leah, the older, and Rachel. Laban promised Jacob that he could marry Rachel, the one he loved, after working for him for seven years, and Jacob worked joyfully because he knew the time was a prelude to marriage with his true love. But when the time came to be married, Laban switched daughters, and Jacob ended up marrying Leah, the older and less attractive daughter. He had worked loyally for Laban and made him wealthy, but Laban just wanted his oldest daughter married first.

King David. The Bible says that David was "a man after God's own heart" (1 Samuel 13:14). He was loyal to King Saul and refused to harm Saul since God had anointed Saul Israel's first king. David was handsome, was a highly successful soldier, and was loved by the people of Israel. However, when his son Absalom made a run at the kingdom, David had to flee from Jerusalem in order to save his own life. He had done so much for all the Hebrew nation, yet when a younger, more handsome replacement showed up, it was as if David was forgotten, and his people had no respect or love for him any longer.

Nazareth. Even a place can be disrespected as is the case regarding Jesus's birthplace. Jesus was just beginning his ministry and in the process of calling His disciples when He came across Nathanael (Bartholomew), a man whom another disciple Philip had told about Jesus. When Nathanael heard that Jesus was from Nazareth he said, "Nazareth! Can anything good come from there?" (John 1:46 NIV). However, this story ended well because of the power Jesus had to touch the lives of those He knew so well. Nathanael was convinced, and the rest, as they say, is history! But the story of Nazareth did not end there, and as this lesson begins, there is a very different story preceding it.

In Mark 6:4 Jesus prophesied by saying, "A prophet is not without honor, except in his hometown and among his relatives in his own household." John 4:44 (a parenthetical expression) says, "For Jesus himself had testified that a prophet has no honor in his hometown." So Jesus, like Moses, Jacob, and King David before Him was rejected by some of those who knew Him best, and as the story continues to unfold, believers know that He was totally rejected by and killed by some of the very people He had come to redeem: the Jewish nation.

How about you? Do you reject the *one* who came to save you because you find this or that wrong with Him or with what He taught? Or do you follow Him and do His will in everything?

STUDY GUIDE

While the opening questions in this lesson are not applicable to the miracle itself, they set the stage for why Jesus was where He was. All too often believers fail to remember all the psychological pain and agony Jesus endured to teach them how to live. Believers know about the physical suffering inflicted upon Him on His final day on earth but may not think of Him as a fully human being who was rejected by His own, even His family who should have loved Him most. For that reason, believers need always remember these words from 1 John 4:19: "We love because He first loved us."

Opening Questions

1. After reading Mark 6:4, find other verse(s) that demonstrate that Jesus did not have honor with His own relatives early in His ministry.

2. Give an example through a Bible verse or book(s) of how Jesus's family eventually came around and gave Him the credit and the honor He deserved.

3. Skim John 4:1–42. What main event was taking place in these verses that occurred close to the miracle in this lesson?

4. With those verses from John 4:1–42 in mind, answer the following:

    a. Give one or more reasons why the Samaritans and Jews were bitter enemies.
    b. What one or more things were unusual in these verses?
    c. What one or more things can be learned about Jesus in these verses?

5. Focus on verse 42 and provide answers to the following questions:

    a. What makes the words in this verse so important to understanding salvation?
    b. What does this say about a believer's role in the kingdom? (Also see Romans 10:17.)

Questions Leading Up to the Performance of the Miracle

Sometimes Jesus is tenderly directing a weak faith. Again, by apparent refusal, He is drawing into view the strength of a strong faith. Another time, He is teaching that the miracle is not the cause of faith so much as its reward; that bodily cures are chiefly of use to bring spiritual help; that belief in Him as a Healer is meant to lead men to faith in Him as a Savior.[12]

6. Read John 4:43–45. What was meant by Jesus's words?

7. What were some things Jesus had done in Jerusalem that are revealed in verse 45?

8. See if you can track Jesus's journey from the time of His baptism to the time of the healing of the official's son in Galilee.

Questions about the Miracle

John 4:46–54

9. By reading commentaries and different versions of the Bible, determine what was likely the religious background of the person who approached Jesus. (John 2:18 and John 4:48 should help with this answer.)

10. The scripture identifies the man as an official. What might the term official have meant in this context?

11. On whom was this miracle performed, and what was the malady?

12. *Challenge.* What important change came over the person between what is said in verse 47 when compared to what is said in verse 50?

[12] John Laidlaw, *The Miracles of Our Lord* (Grand Rapids: Zondervan, 1961), 164.

13. *Challenge.* What reveals that the official had gained an enormous amount of faith in Jesus's healing power?

14. Why did the official ask his servant what time his son began to improve, and why was that another seminal point in the official's life?

15. Like the earlier question asked in 5b, what does this miracle say about a believer's role in the kingdom?

16. What does this statement from Herbert Lockyer in *All the Miracles of the Bible* mean to you as a believer in the world today? "While the nobleman's [the official's] sorrow was the birth-pang of faith, he revealed the limit of that faith when he limited the power of Christ to His local presence."[13]

Summary Questions

17. The scripture for this lesson is the first recording of a specific type of activity of Jesus, and it is important for many reasons, but one of the main points of importance is that it links the type of activity with an absolute requirement of the Christian life.

    a. What is that type of activity? (Don't overthink this!)
    b. What is that requirement of the Christian life?

18. How did this miracle affect the one who performed it?

---

[13] Herbert Lockyer, "The Miracle of the Nobleman's Son," in All *the Miracles of the Bible* (Grand Rapids: Zondervan Publishing House, 1961), 163–165.

19. How did this miracle affect the person on whom the miracle was performed?

20. How did this miracle affect the person who sought it? (Look beyond just the individual.)

21. What is the spiritual sign to which this miracle pointed?

22. Think about Jesus's two most used teaching methods: miracles and parables. John 2:23 (NLT) says, "Because of the miraculous signs Jesus did in Jerusalem at the Passover celebration, many began to trust in him." In other places in the New Testament, after teaching a parable, Jesus said, "He who has ears, let him hear." Therefore, in your opinion, which of the teaching methods of Jesus was more effective? Why?

Faith in a wrong object, no matter how strong, never relieves; but faith in a right object, although weak, will. It is not faith itself that relieves, but the power of the One in whom we believe.[14]

[14] Lockyer, 164.

LESSON 4

Jesus Drives an Evil Spirit from a Man

When one thinks about the birth of the Christian church, it would not be unlikely that those thoughts would turn to Acts 2 when Peter, the rock of the church, gave the first heartfelt sermon that was inspired by God and led by the Holy Spirit. Toward the end of the message that Peter taught to the crowd, he said to the throng that had joined to listen, "Let all the house of Israel therefore know for certain that God has made him both Lord and Christ, this Jesus whom you crucified" (Acts 2:36).

So a question might be asked once all of Peter's sermon has been read—a question that might go something like this, "Was this the first salvo at the beginning of a new faith that was instituted by Christ's birth, ministry, death, and resurrection?" Many Christians read the Old Testament, close it out with the last words from Malachi, and see it as Act 1 of God's story (see Malachi 4:5–6) Then beginning in Matthew, those same Christians get all excited about Act 2 when Jesus came on the scene and began His ministry of the New Testament Church. However, pause a minute and look at what Peter said in the quote above.

Peter had just quoted things spoken in the writings of David, and David was one of the most revered Jews of the ages. Peter then started the wrap-up of his sermon by saying, "Therefore." When the Bible uses a word like that, the author is linking what has come before the word and what will come after it. Consequently, Peter wanted those listening to him to understand that his message was connecting a hero of the Jewish people, David, with what he was going to say next, "let all Israel be assured of this." What can be made of that? Peter wanted the listeners of his sermon to know that what the Jews knew all along had happened! It was not a new story; it was simply a continuation of what had been for 4,000 years and would be for all eternity. What evidence is there of that?

First, consider where Jesus often taught when He wanted to get His message across to the most possible people. He taught in the synagogues or the temple, the place where the Jewish leaders and the Jewish population would go to worship God. If Jesus were trying to start something new, why would He have taken His message to the "same old crowd"?

Second, when Jesus began His message on any given Sabbath in a synagogue or the Temple, how did He grab the attention of His listeners? He did not start from scratch with something new and unique, but rather, He always began with a reading from the Hebrew scriptures taken directly from the holy scrolls that were a part of the Jewish houses of worship.

Third, and most importantly, what did Jesus say that He had come to do—or more precisely—what He had come not to do? In Matthew 5:17, during the Sermon on the Mount, Jesus made this very bold statement, "Do not think that I have come to abolish the Law or the Prophets; I have not come to abolish them but to fulfill them." That does not sound like a statement someone would make if that person were trying to do something new and different!

The synagogue and the Temple were the places where Jesus

saw some of His greatest successes, and they were also the places where He felt some of the most difficult challenges from those He came to help. But as with all things He faced, He faced them head-on without apology—telling the truth. He wanted people to understand that the scriptures were to be taken in by the heart and not just by the mind, and He wanted them to know that a loving relationship with Him and with others is what is really important.

STUDY GUIDE

The 37 miracles of Jesus Christ that were written down in the New Testament serve a specific purpose. None were performed randomly, for amusement, or for show. Each was accompanied by a message and either met a serious human need or confirmed Christ's identity and authority as the Son of God. At times Jesus refused to perform miracles because they did not fall into one of these two categories.[15]

After reading the quote above, can you find a specific time in the Bible when Jesus refused to perform a miracle because it did not meet the criteria listed in the quote?

Opening Questions

1. The town of Capernaum is mentioned sixteen times in the King James Version of the Bible, all in the four Gospels. See what facts you can find out about Capernaum and why that city may

[15] Mary Fairchild, "Miracles of Jesus: From Healing the Sick to Turning Water Into Wine" (updated December 05, 2022), https://www.learnreligions.com/miracles-of-jesus-700158.

have been so important to Christ's ministry. There are both positive and negative reasons.

2. This is a two-part question about the teachings of Jesus.

    a. The end of Mark 1:22 says, "He taught them as one who had authority, and not as the scribes." What do you think Mark meant when he wrote those words, particularly as it applied to the scribes?
    b. *Challenge.* When you study God's Word, what is something that astonishes you about the teachings of Jesus?

3. What one or more things should one be able to determine by the fact that Jesus taught in the synagogues wherever He went?

Questions Leading Up to the Performance of the Miracle

4. The book of Mark is filled with short, clipped statements that are full of action words. What point or points do you think he was making by writing with this particular style?

5. Why is it significant that the interaction with the man with the unclean spirit happened on the Sabbath?

6. Read the quote below. In your opinion, if the devil is the prince of this world, meaning that God has given him great power, why has God done that even though He could have easily said, "You're done!"?

Satan and demons have great power (compared to humans). Even Michael the archangel trusts only God's power when dealing with Satan (Jude 1:9). But Satan's power is nothing compared to God's (Acts 19:11–12, Mark 5:1–20), and God is able to use Satan's evil intent to bring about His good purposes (1 Corinthians 5:5, 2 Corinthians 12:7).[16]

Questions about the Miracle

Mark 1:21–28

7. Verse 23 says, "And immediately there was in their synagogue a man with an unclean spirit." What do you think those few words are trying to tell the reader?

8. How do you think an unclean spirit was able to enter a holy place such as the synagogue?

9. Verses 23 and 24 have no less than three important statements that are made by the evil spirit. Look at those below and give your impression of what they mean.

    a. "And he cried out, 'What have you to do with us?'"
    b. "Have you come to destroy us?"
    c. "I know who you are—the Holy One of God!"

10. In verse 24 above the unclean spirit speaks directly to Jesus, yet in verse 25 Jesus tells the unclean spirit to be quiet. Since the unclean spirit had said that he knew Jesus was the Holy One of

---

16 "Is there activity of demonic spirits in the world today?," https://www.gotquestions.org/demonic-activity.html.

God, why did Jesus tell him to be silent? How does this agree with or conflict with Luke 9:50?

11. What effort was taken on Jesus's part to get rid of the unclean spirit, and what does that say about our Savior?

12. *Challenge.* Commentator Lockyer in his book *All the Miracles of the Bible* demonstrates that this miracle illustrates Jesus's lordship over at least three different areas of life or places.[17] Which of those can you find that is demonstrated in these eight short verses?

    a. Area 1
    b. Area 2
    c. Area 3

Summary Questions

13. Lockyer says, "Jesus was often weary IN His work but never weary OF it."[18] After looking at John 4:6, explain what you think Lockyer meant.

14. How did this miracle affect the one who performed the miracle?

15. How did this miracle affect the one on whom the miracle was performed?

16. How did this miracle affect those who witnessed the miracle?

---

[17] Lockyer, "The Miracle of the Synagogue Demonic," 168–170.

[18] Lockyer, 168.

17. Is there anything about this miracle that is convicting or gives you pause to think a bit deeper about the majesty of the Lord?

18. Read the quote below. Is there anything you can offer from your personal experience that would either verify or contradict what is said?

Have we anything today answering to the demon in the synagogue? Has history repeated itself? We think it has. When in buildings erected for the preaching of the inspired, infallible scriptures, preachers discredit the reliability of the Bible, repudiate the miracles, flout the virgin birth, the atoning blood, and the physical resurrection of Christ, what are they with all their education and polish but demons in the synagogue? As they do not represent the spirit of truth, some other spirit must possess them.[19]

[19] Lockyer, 169.

LESSON 5

Jesus Heals Peter's Mother-in-Law's Fever
Jesus Heals the Oppressed and the Sick

A great deal can be learned about the *providence of God* in a book titled *Confessing the Faith* by Chad Van Dixhoorn. Before getting into any comments about miracles, it seems fitting to share some information from the book since God's providence is tremendously important to understanding the world and understanding the mystery of how the providence of God works. Try as one might, it won't ever be understood completely just because it is so mysterious! The point at which Van Dixhoorn is quoted begins with the following words,

> We may forget this sometimes when we complain about our smaller problems or forget to praise God for our smaller blessings. But the fact remains, as Jesus reminded His disciples, that all things are under God's control, "from the greatest even to the least." All things are under God's direction, even the sparrow sadly dropping from the sky; even the hair sadly dropping from our heads (Matthew 10:29–31).

> All providence is God's "most wise and holy providence." We can trust him and know that he is right. Of course, this providence is "most wise and holy" (Proverbs 15:3; Psalm 104:24; Psalm 145:17) because it is in perfect harmony with God's "infallible foreknowledge" (Acts 15:18; Psalm 94:8–11), and "the free, and immutable counsel of His own will" (Ephesians 1:11).[20]

So how do the subject of God's providence and Jesus's miracles have anything to do with one another? This is best explained by looking at the surface of another miracle, the miracle of Jesus raising from the dead the son of the widow of Nain, which will be studied later in lesson 11.

Jesus had just completed a successful ministry campaign, and there were as many as a hundred people who continued to follow Him and listen to Him as He and His disciples traveled about twenty-five miles from the town of Capernaum to the town of Nain. Jesus and His disciples were walking, talking, and celebrating; in effect, they were joyous in the light of what Messiah had said to them. As they reached the very outskirts of Nain, coming toward them was another crowd, but this one was sad. They were mourning because the widow of Nain's son had died and because there was no longer a male in her household, so she would be facing a life of uncertainty and perhaps destitution. Certainly, there was sadness over the death of the son, but perhaps there was even greater sadness about what

[20] Chad Van Dixhorn, *Confessing the Faith* (Edinburgh: Banner of Truth. 2014), 68.

the future held for this woman. In His providence, God brought these two groups together.

As Jesus and His party came into town, the widow of Nain and the funeral procession were going out of town. They met and that was when the miracle occurred: Jesus raised the widow's son to new life, and with her son restored, she was assured of having a male to take care of her. Just think if Jesus had been five minutes later or if the widow had been five minutes later, the two would not have met, and the story would have had a different and sad ending. While those who do not believe would call this a coincidence, there is no such thing for the believer. This was providential; God's hand was working to make these two groups meet one another!

Two sons met that day, one of them, Jesus, was destined to die while the other was destined to live. Two sufferers met that day, Jesus the man of sorrows, and the woman who had lost her son. And, finally, two enemies met--life and death. But because of God's providence, this story ends well, and the story of Jesus ends well too—particularly for believers who call Him Savior!

STUDY GUIDE

Jesus's fame was increasing. His ministry had begun with the calling of His disciples. Now Jesus traveled with them in the region of Galilee, teaching and performing miracles. The people recognized that Jesus wasn't like other teachers; He taught with authority. He had even demonstrated His power over unclean spirits by healing a man in the synagogue. News about Jesus was spreading. The subject of conversation around Galilee was changing. Who was this Jesus?[21]

Is there anything in the opening thoughts or in the quote above that might convict, intrigue, or cause disagreement?

Opening Questions

1. This study of Jesus's miracles is scheduled to look at many of His thirty-seven miracles recorded in the Bible. Jesus taught for about three years. Do you think thirty-seven miracles are all He performed? Why or why not? Give biblical support for your answer.

2. "The miracles of Jesus range from changing water into wine to healing the lame and the blind. How do we know He did these things? We have the eyewitness testimony of four gospel writers."[22] With that in mind, what are some reasons people had, in the time of Jesus and have currently, not to believe what the Gospel writers wrote?

Questions Leading Up to the Performance of the Miracle

This is a simple story about an unpretentious woman, Peter's mother-in-law. She is nameless because the focus of the story is

[21] "Jesus Healed Peter's Mother-in-Law," accessed March 1, 2019, https://www.gileadfriendschurch.org/jesus-healed-peters-mother-in-law.html.

[22] "Miracles of Jesus," accessed March 1, 2019, https://www.allaboutjesuschrist.org/miracles-of-jesus-.htm.

on Jesus's miracle, not on her. Yet her story has been told in all Christian lands.[23]

3. Read Matthew 4:18–20. When read in conjunction with Matthew 8:14, what new perspective might one get regarding Jesus's call of Peter and Peter's response? You will have to "read between the lines."

4. Considering that Jesus was fully human, what might He have been looking forward to as He entered the house of Peter?

Questions about the Miracles

Matthew 8:14–17 (also in Mark 1:29–34 and Luke 4:38–41)

5. *Jesus Heals Peter's Mother-in-law's Fever.* Read the version of this miracle in Matthew, Mark, and Luke and then answer the following questions:

    a. What two key facts does Luke include in his gospel, verses 38 and 39, that Matthew and Mark do not? Note: These differences are found in the ESV; they may or may not be as clear in other versions.
    b. Why was it fitting that Luke in particular mentioned the first point?
    c. What might one be able to tell about the illness based on what Luke said in the first point?

---

[23] "Jesus Heals Peter's Mother-In-Law," accessed March 1, 2019, https://www.livingwordlightoflife.com/jesus-heals-peters-mother-in-law.

d. What can one tell about the nature of the mother-in-law's illness from the second point?

6. *Jesus Heals Peter's Mother-in-law's Fever.* There is also something unique mentioned in the Matthew and Mark versions of this miracle. What is that, and why is that so unique?

7. *Jesus Heals Peter's Mother-in-law's Fever.* What, if anything, does that (the answer to question 6 above) say about Jesus and His power to heal?

8. *Jesus Heals Peter's Mother-in-law's Fever.* Do you see any special significance that this miracle was held in a private home?

9. *Jesus Heals the Oppressed and the Sick.* What other miracles did Jesus perform in these verses?

10. *Jesus Heals the Oppressed and the Sick.* What does the answer to question 9 tell you about Jesus?

11. *Jesus Heals the Oppressed and the Sick.* Isaiah 53:4 is quoted in the scriptures for this lesson, and Isaiah was written between 739 and 681 BC which means that it was written between 769 and 711 years before the ministry of Jesus. With that in mind, answer the following questions.

    a. Why is it important to know that?
    b. What does that say about the Bible?

Summary Questions

12. The miracle of the demoniac in the temple in the previous lesson and the two miracles from this lesson were all done on the same day. What does that say about Jesus?

13. All that is known about Peter's mother-in-law is found in the verses from the three gospels of Matthew, Mark and Luke. With such little information, what can be told about serving the Lord?

14. According to one source, there are two firsts for Jesus in these verses. Try to figure out what those two firsts were.

15. How did these miracles affect the people on whom they were performed?

16. How did these miracles affect the people who witnessed them?

17. Dr. A. E. Garvie concludes an article in Hasting's *Dictionary of the Bible* by saying, "At the beginning of the Christian Church the miracles had some value as evidence."

    a. Of what were the miracles serving as evidence?
    b. Why would miracles have been needed as evidence?
    c. Why is not the same type of evidence needed today?

18. What is the most meaningful lesson to be learned from these two miracles?

    a. Jesus's Heals Peter's Mother-in-law's Fever
    b. Jesus's Heals the Oppressed and the Sick

Although miracles may not happen today as they did in Jesus's time, the time of the first apostles, and the time of the first-century church, read what Lockyer has to say about miracles today in his book, *All the Miracles of the Bible.* "Before (dismissing) the question of the cessation or continuation of miracles, it must be made clear that we are not asserting that God does not exert His supernatural power today when and where a miracle is necessary. As the omnipotent One, He does not change; and there are faithful, reliable Christians who ... have experienced that there is still nothing too hard for the Lord."[24]

---

[24] Lockyer, "The Miracle of Peter's Mother-in-Law," 170–171.

LESSON 6
First Miracle of Catching Fish

Miracles can be studied every week. Individuals can determine what they think miracles are all about, but there are many who are more qualified to discuss miracles than the average layperson. Getting some quotes about miracles from familiar authors is a good place to start. The following is a very abbreviated list of what some well-known authors have said over the years.

"Some people probably think of the Resurrection as a desperate last moment expedient to save the Hero from a situation which had got out of the Author's control" (C. S. Lewis).

"Miracles are not contrary to nature, but only contrary to what we know about nature" (Augustine).

"The gospel which they so greatly needed they would not have; the miracles which Jesus did not always choose to give, they eagerly demanded" (Charles Spurgeon).

"Miracles are a retelling in small letters of the very same story which is written across the whole world in letters too large for some of us to see" (C. S. Lewis).

"When human reason has exhausted every possibility, the children can go to their Father and receive all they need. ... For only when you have become utterly dependent upon prayer and faith, only when all human possibilities have been exhausted, can you begin to reckon that God will intervene and work His miracles" (Basilea Schlink).

"How quickly we forget God's great deliverances in our lives. How easily we take for granted the miracles he performed in our past" (David Wilkerson).

"I never have any difficulty believing in miracles since I experienced the miracle of a change in my own heart" (Augustine).

"The whole order of things is as outrageous as any miracle which could presume to violate it" (G. K. Chesterton).

"Christ's miracles were not the suspension of the natural order but the restoration of the natural order. They were a reminder of what once was prior to the fall and a preview of what will eventually be a universal reality once again—a world of peace and justice, without death, disease, or conflict" (Tim Keller).

"Prophecy and miracles argue the imperfection of the state of the church, rather than its perfection. For they are means designed by God as a stay or support, or as a leading to the church in its infancy, rather than as means adapted to it in its full growth" (Jonathan Edwards)

These quotes are just a small sampling of what is available on the internet. These all come from www.christianquotes.info.[25] They are all intriguing in one way or another, but they all help give a clearer understanding of what miracles are and have been. What would your quote about miracles be? Compose a quote in the first question of the lesson, and maybe your quote will end up becoming famous someday! But if not famous, it will certainly be meaningful to you and the rest of those with whom you study.

---

25 "Miracles," accessed March 1, 2019, https://www.christianquotes.info/search/miracles.

STUDY GUIDE

"The twelve disciples/apostles were ordinary men whom God used in an extraordinary manner. Among the twelve were fishermen, a tax collector, and a revolutionary. The Gospels record the constant failings, struggles, and doubts of these twelve men who followed Jesus Christ." [26] First, would anyone in a hiring capacity have chosen these men for a business, especially in roles of leadership? Second, how many of them would have been kept around after their "constant failings, struggles, and doubts?" It is wonderful that God is in control and not mankind!

Read the quote above. Are there one or more points that stand out and/or are particularly meaningful to you?

Opening Questions

1. *Challenge.* Compose your own quote about miracles.

2. Jesus did not call His disciples to follow Him on His first encounter with them. In fact, there may have been at least two previous meetings with some of the original twelve before any of them were called for their special role. Why would it have taken Jesus more than one meeting to make the call that He made to Peter, James, and John in the verses for tonight's lesson? (Luke 5:1–11).

3. What characteristics of a fisherman would complement the skills that would be required to be a disciple of the Lord?

---

[26] gotquestions.org, "Who were the twelve (12) apostles/disciples of Jesus Christ?," https://www.gotquestions.org/twelve-apostles-disciples-12.html

Questions Leading Up to the Performance of the Miracle

Luke 5:1–3

4. Where is Lake Gennesaret, and what is another name for it?

5. Read Luke 5:1–2 and give as much information as you can about what is taking place.

    a. What is important to you?
    b. What sticks out from the two verses?
    c. Is there anything that is particularly convicting or encouraging?

6. After reading verse 3, tell what Jesus did and explain why you think he did what He did.

Questions about the Miracle

Luke 5:4–11

7. Read Luke 5:4–5 and answer the following questions:

    a. What did Jesus tell Simon to do?
    b. From a fishing standpoint, why was this an unusual request?
    c. What was Simon's first response?
    d. What was Simon's second response?
    e. What does this interaction between Jesus and Simon tell us?

   i. about Jesus
   ii. about Simon

8. What is the spiritual significance of the large haul of fish?

9. What is the spiritual significance of asking the men in the other boats to help with the haul?

10. Why did Simon say what he said in verse 8?

11. Why do you think this event came to be a turning point in the lives of the disciples named in this passage (Simon, James, and John), particularly Simon?

12. The three men mentioned in the previous question became the inner circle of the Lord. Why would those three have had an elevated status with Jesus? (Think about the omniscience of Jesus and what He knew about the future for each of them.)

    a. Simon
    b. James
    c. John

Summary Questions

13. Briefly state the meaning of this miracle in your own words.

14. How did this miracle affect the one who performed the miracle?

15. How did it affect the one for whom the miracle was performed?

16. How did it affect those who witnessed the miracle?

We ask God for many things, but the greatest thing we could ever receive from him has already been given. What God has given us in the gospel is light-years ahead of every other provision and care we could ever seek from him. When we trust in Christ, we have decisively secured for us every ultimately good thing from him. It's just a matter of time.[27]

17. Read the quote above and then answer the following questions:

    a. Why do you think the author refers to the Gospel as the "greatest thing we could ever receive from him"?
    b. The author also said, "When we trust in Christ, we have decisively secured for us every ultimately good thing from him."

        i. Why does he use the word decisively? Can you provide a Bible verse or verses that verify what he means?
        ii. What would you include in "every ultimately good thing from him"?

[27] "Four Truths About God's Provision," accessed March 1, 2019, https://www.desiringgod.org/articles/four-truths-about-gods-provision.

LESSON 7

Jesus Cleanses a Man with Leprosy

In review look at some of the important aspects of the miracles studied in Lessons 2 through 6.

- *Jesus Changes Water to Wine.* While seemingly insignificant in some ways, this was the first miracle performed by Jesus. It helped Jesus's mother Mary get a better understanding of who her son was, and it showed how Jesus could always provide the best of everything as He did when changing the water to the very best wine.

- *Jesus Heals the Official's Son.* There is no knowledge of who the official was, but it is known that he had faith in Jesus since he asked Him to heal his son. This miracle also showed that there was no need to be physically present to make His miracles happen.

- *Jesus Drives Out an Evil Spirit.* What is learned from this miracle is that even the evil spirits that attack people are not strong enough to defeat the Savior. This was Jesus's first confrontation with such a spirit, but it will not be His last. And He always wins the day!

- *Jesus Heals Peter's Mother-in-law.* There are two nuanced lessons in this miracle. First, it reveals that at least one of the original twelve disciples was married. Second, it shows that when Jesus cured someone, that person was healed immediately—there was no waiting period.

- *First Miraculous Catch of Fish.* Jesus's miracles were not limited to just people or spirits, but He demonstrated that He also had power over the physical world. It also showed fishermen turned disciples that they would need to work together if they were to fish for men effectively.

By performing miracles, Jesus was demonstrating that there were no limits to His power. In today's world, people question not only the power to perform miracles, but they question miracles themselves. Miracles such as those performed by the Lord and then by the apostles in the first-century church ended with the apostles' ministry. However, this does not mean that God is not working in miraculous ways today. Consider the quote below.

> We do not mean by this that God does not answer prayers today or that His supernatural work does not continue. We see people healed in response to prayer and converted by His Spirit. Yet we also need to think about the proper distinction between miracles and His ongoing supernatural works. Theologians have a strict definition of miracles, as Dr. R. C. Sproul explains: A miracle, properly speaking, is an "extraordinary work performed by the immediate power of God in the external perceivable world, which is an act against nature

> that only God can do" (for example, resurrections and floating axe heads). Considered this way, it seems clear that miracles are not occurring in the present.[28]

Miracles such as those performed by Jesus and the apostles no longer occur, but that doesn't mean that God doesn't do miraculous work in the world today. He is with us every step of the way, and He has provided the Holy Spirit to go on our walk with us. God's plan to restore His people to Himself is going exactly as planned—and that will never change.

STUDY GUIDE

An amazing 115 verses in chapters 13 and 14 of Leviticus deal with the purification of those people who had leprosy! While *leprosy* was a catch-all phrase for many diseases, even for mold and mildew in homes, it was obviously a serious issue for the Israelites because God is the one who told Moses how leprosy was to be handled and what would happen to leprous people considered unclean according to the priests. Therefore, in the minds of God's people, the term leprosy was not to be toyed with, and the results of being a leper could be disastrous, physically, socially, and spiritually.

[28] "Does R. C. Sproul Believe in Miracles?," accessed March 1, 2019, https://www.ligonier.org/learn/articles/does-rcsproul-believe-miracles.

Opening Questions

1. *Challenge.* Think for a few minutes about Moses and Jesus. Using your Bible, your personal knowledge, and other resources, see what similarities can be found between the two men.

2. Consider the whole Bible and share what you know or can find out about two or three of the most prominent lepers in the Bible. Most of them will be from the Old Testament.

3. Are there any diseases today that create similar fear and/or revulsion toward people as leprosy in Jesus's day?

Questions Leading Up to the Performance of the Miracle

4. What do you know about the life of a leper and the general view of lepers in biblical times, especially as recorded in the Old Testament?

5. Matthew places this miracle immediately after the conclusion of the Sermon on the Mount. Why would he do that?

6. The Jews called leprosy "the finger of God." What does that imply with respect to the disease?

Questions about the Miracle

Mark 1:40–45 (also Matthew 8:1–4, Luke 5:12–15)

7. The English Standard Version (ESV) of the Bible indicates the man was in a kneeling position while other versions say he fell to his knees, or he fell on his face. Regardless of the descriptions used, what one thing is indicated by the various positions?

8. In his Gospel, Luke says this particular leper was a man full of leprosy. Knowing that Luke was a physician, why did he use that language?

9. Note that the man said, "If you will, you can make me clean." Why do you think he asked to be made clean rather than to be healed?

10. How does the leper in this miracle demonstrate the following:

    a. faith
    b. distrust

11. What is most striking to you in each of the following verses? Why?

    a. verse 40
    b. verse 41
    c. verse 42

12. Based on verses 44 and 45, answer the following questions:

    a. Why did Jesus tell the leper to tell no one about the miraculous healing?

b. Why did the man intentionally disobey the Lord?
c. What were the negative consequences of the man's disobedience?

Summary Questions

13. *Challenge.* Herbert Lockyer in his book *All the Miracles of the Bible* makes this powerful statement: "When we accept the truth of His lordship, there is no difficulty in crediting Him with almightiness."[29] What does that statement mean to you?

14. What is the main message Mark wanted people to get from this miracle? As you answer this, keep in mind how totally devastating this disease was to those who had it.

15. Is there anything about the miracle that convicts and/or encourages you?

16. How did the miracle affect the following:

    a. the one who performed the miracle
    b. the one on whom the miracle was performed
    c. those who witnessed the miracle

When Jesus performed miracles, He often told the recipient of the miracle to not tell anyone. In this modern world of telling everyone every little thing ever accomplished, this might not make any sense. However, see what gotquestions.org says about why Jesus did what He did.

[29] Lockyer, "The Miracle of the Leper Cleansed," 173.

To our way of thinking, it would seem that Jesus would want everyone to know about the miracle. But Jesus knew that publicity over such miracles might hinder His mission and divert public attention from His message. Mark records that this is exactly what happened. In this man's (the leper) excitement over his being miraculously healed, he disobeyed. As a result, Christ had to move His ministry away from the city and into the desert regions (Mark 1:45). "As a result, Jesus could no longer enter a town openly but stayed outside in lonely places. Yet the people still came to Him from everywhere."

In addition, Christ, though he had cleansed the leper, still required him to be obedient to the law of the land—to go at once to the priest, and not to make delay by stopping to converse about his being healed. It was also possible that, if he did not go at once, evil-minded men would go before him and prejudice the priest and prevent his declaring the healing to be true because it was done by Jesus. It was of further importance that the priest should pronounce it to be a genuine cure, that there might be no prejudice among the Jews against its being a real miracle.

Finally, Jesus did not want people focusing on the miracles He performed, but rather the message He proclaimed and the death He was going to die. The same is true today. God would rather that we be focused on the healing miracle of salvation through Jesus Christ instead of focusing on other healings and/or miracles.[30]

[30] "Why did Jesus command people to not tell others of the miracles He performed?" https://gotquestions.org/do-not-tell.html.

LESSON 8

Jesus Heals the Centurion's Servant

In the 1980s and 1990s, there was a disease that was spreading fear into the hearts of a certain population both in the United States and in the world. The human immunodeficiency virus, if not treated, led to what was and is known as AIDS (acquired immunodeficiency syndrome). The population that was first threatened by the disease was the gay community, but due to the ways AIDS was transmitted, drug addicts and those who received blood transfusions became infected as well. While the death rate from the disease was drastic enough, the biggest enemy was the absolute fear it put into a person when diagnosed with AIDS.

Compare that disease with the COVID-19 virus that spread throughout the world beginning in 2020. Millions of people were affected and millions died, yet the worst part of the disease was the fear that people all over the world experienced. People were quarantined, stores were closed, people couldn't eat in restaurants, and everyone was required to wear a mask and take other protective measures that were ordered by the governments of various nations.

Consider those two diseases in comparison to *leprosy* in the Bible. If a person got leprosy, he or she was not only sick and would waste away but was also totally ostracized from their community.

They had to live outside the city, they could have no contact with their families, they had no way to make a living, and they were declared unclean, which meant touching them in any way was forbidden. Additionally, for the Jews of Jesus's time, a leper could not attend the synagogue. But the really big difference between leprosy and AIDS or COVID-19 was that there was no medical science to combat its effects or spread.

However, Jesus entered the world stage and demonstrated His willingness to deal with the leper as a real person who needed healing. In fact, Jesus was so loving that He did not mind coming near them and even touching them. Certainly, they needed physical healing, but Jesus realized that more than that, they needed spiritual healing. Fortunately for them, He could provide them with both. As with many good things, however, there was a negative side to this healing and to other of His healings.

His enemies—the Pharisees, Sadducees, priests, scribes, and the rest of the ruling class of the Jews—looked for every opportunity possible to find fault with Jesus. These were the very people that Jesus came to save by showing them the true way to the Father, but they were not interested in that. They were interested in holding on to their power, their prestige, their wealth, and their reputation within the community. They saw Jesus as a threat. Jesus was on earth to create a new kind of kingdom, but His enemies were quite happy with the way things were.

Throughout Jesus's ministry, there were all sorts of ways the Jews in power tried to make him out to be a blasphemer and an agent of Satan. These attacks were not just limited to the miracles, and the leaders of the Jews used every opportunity possible to discredit Jesus. There were notable exceptions among these leaders such as Joseph of Arimathea and Nicodemus, but the exceptions were rare. But while the Jewish leaders were doing everything to destroy Him, what He was doing in His ministry continued to win over those who had no real power.

That continues to be the way it is. Those in power are always the ones who want their way and will try to do whatever it takes to hold on to their power, but true power only belongs to Jesus.

STUDY GUIDE

Opening Questions

1. There is value in regularly reflecting on what true faith looks like. Give two or three examples of men or women from the Bible that exemplify, in your mind, true faith. Your answer should exclude the centurion in this lesson. Name the person, the situation, and why the faith story impresses you.

2. Similarly, come up with one or more examples of men or women in the Bible who did not demonstrate true faith in the Lord. If possible, use an example of someone who was a follower of the Lord at first. Name the person, the situation, and the outcome of the fall from faith.

Questions Leading Up to the Performance of the Miracle

3. As a refresher and reminder, what one or more important facts do you know about Capernaum?

4. Read Luke 7:1 along with Matthew 8:1, and then answer the following questions:

    a. What event is being referred to when Luke wrote, "He had finished all his sayings in the hearing of the people"?
    b. What did you find out about the crowd that had been listening to Jesus when you read Matthew 8:1? (Think beyond the simple statement made in this verse.)

Questions about the Miracle

Luke 7:1–10 (also Matthew 8:5–13)

5. Why is it so important that the person in this miracle is identified as a centurion? There may be one or more points that distinguish Him.

6. Verse 3 says the centurion had heard about Jesus. Those words prompt at least two questions:

    a. How do you think that the centurion heard about Jesus?
    b. What does this say about Jesus's ministry at this point in time?

7. Why would the centurion, a Gentile, work with the Jewish leadership to try to get his servant healed? And why would the Jews have been willing to help the Gentiles?

8. *Challenge.* Read Matthew 8:11 along with Luke 7:4–5. What important point, said in different ways, is being taught in these two passages of the scripture?

9. The centurion drew a comparison between Jesus and himself in Mathew 8:9 and Luke 7:8. What did the centurion say about himself, and how did that apply to Jesus?

10. One resource says that Matthew and Luke record no less than four distinguishable traits in the character of the centurion. What traits do you see?

11. There are some similarities between Matthew's and Luke's accounts, and one of the most significant is what is recorded in Matthew 8:10 when Jesus says, "Truly, I tell you, with no one in Israel have I found such faith." What point do you think Jesus was making with that statement? (Note: This is the only time in the Bible that Jesus made such a strong statement about the faith of a person.)

12. What special quality (or qualities) of Jesus's healing power is demonstrated in this miracle?

13. Do the verses in Matthew 5:43–48 support the meaning of this lesson's miracle? Whether yes or no, explain your answer.

Summary Questions

14. What do you see as the main point of this miracle?

15. Is there anything that convicts or encourages you through the words of the miracle?

16. How did this miracle affect the person on whom it was performed?

17. How did this miracle affect the person who sought it?

18. Read the quote below. What point or points are most important to you? Explain why those points are important.

This centurion is also a reminder to us that "man looks on the outward appearance, but the Lord looks on the heart" (1 Samuel 16:7). I think we will be surprised someday when Jesus doles out rewards. Most of the great ones among us will probably have lived in obscurity. Jesus is not as impressed with titles, degrees, and achievements as we are. He is impressed with those who really do humbly believe him.[31]

[31] "The Centurion: Faith that Made Jesus Marvel," https://www.desiringgod.org/articles/the-centurion-faith-that-made-jesus-marvel.

LESSON 9
Jesus Heals a Paralytic

What was a centurion in the time of Jesus? The best way to describe what a centurion was is to isolate a few points as to how a man became one and what he did when he achieved that level.

1. Centurions were pulled from the ranks of soldiers within the Roman army.

2. They were tapped for the position because of their bravery, loyalty, character, and prowess in battle.

3. A senior centurion was in a position of great prestige.

4. Each centurion commanded a platoon of men known as a century.

5. A century could be anything from nearly a hundred soldiers to several hundred.

6. The centurion fought with the men under him, and they all fought at the very front of the line.

7. Because of all these, they were paid well, were held in high esteem, and were influential in society.

Why is it important that these points are made about a centurion in the time of Jesus? First, all centurions were obviously Roman. Second, they were seen by those below them as the Romans' Romans. And last, since they were Romans and loyal to the nation of Rome, they would have seen Caesar as being both the head of state and a god. They would have had no need for the foolishness of the god of the Jews, and if they had, they would not have survived very long.

And yet the centurion in the previous lesson had not only become a friend of the Jewish leaders by helping them build their synagogue, but he had also reached out to Jesus, the Son of God, the one who was God incarnate. In more modern times, that might be compared to a soldier in the German army of World War II helping the Jews and then reaching out to the Jewish god rather than worshiping Adolf Hitler who was seen as godlike by many of his blind followers.

But that was the power of Jesus. Even though the Jewish hierarchy did not believe in Him, He could touch the hearts and souls of the common man as well as the hearts and souls of the most heroic of all the Roman soldiers. The centurion saw the similarities between Jesus and himself, and that is part of the reason he turned to Jesus. Whatever the reason, he must have become a believer after the miraculous healing— much the same as what another centurion at the base of the cross witnessed.

> To really grasp who the Savior is today, Christians need to grasp who the Savior was then. He was God's Son sent to earth to do what had been prophesied in

> Isaiah: "Then the eyes of the blind shall be opened, and the ears of the deaf unstopped; then shall the lame man leap like a deer, and the tongue of the mute sing for joy. For waters break forth in the wilderness, and streams in the desert" (Isaiah 35:5–6 ESV).

The miracle in this lesson shows exactly how Jesus filled that prophecy that was written hundreds of years before He was born. A paralyzed man, who had to depend on friends to get him into the presence of the Lord, was soon going to "leap like a deer." It is hard to believe that someone had that kind of power, but Jesus did, and the truth of prophecy was fulfilled many times during Jesus's time on earth. How the people living in Jesus's time must have marveled at what He could do, and believers marvel still today and know that someday all illnesses and deformities will be healed!

STUDY GUIDE

Opening Questions

8. In a study of the attributes of God, two that stand out are His *omniscience* and His *omnipotence.* Since both of those will come into play in this lesson, provide either your own definition or a definition from another source for omniscience and omnipotence.

9. Look at a list of the attributes of God and pick one from that list that is extremely important to you—one that is different than the two in question 1 above. Explain why you chose it.

(The internet is full of lists of God's attributes, but a good one is by Steven Lawson with fifteen attributes.)

Questions Leading Up to the Performance of the Miracle

10. Read John 1:19 along with Luke 5:17, and then answer the following questions:

    a. What is the primary similarity between the verses from John and Luke?
    b. What one or more reasons would the Jewish leadership have done what they did? One of the reasons is probably very legitimate while the other might be seen as conspiratorial.

11. Luke 5:17 also says the following: "And the power of the Lord was with him to heal." Since, not if, Christ was God incarnate, why do you think Jesus had to have the "power of the Lord" with Him to do anything?

Questions about the Miracle

Luke 5:17–26 (also Matthew 9:1–8, Mark 2:1–12)

12. There are several points that are important in this miracle; one of the most interesting is that there is no indication that the paralyzed man ever professed faith in Christ.

a. That seems contrary to the notion that one must come personally to the Lord, doesn't it? Explain your answer.
b. Since the faith of the four men seems to have been the force behind the miracle, what does that say about expectations for believers?
c. Depending on what you answered for question 5b above, when have you last done what is expected of you as a Christian?

13. Look back at your definition of *omniscience* and *omnipotence* in the first question of this lesson. Which of those attributes is demonstrated in verse 20 and which is demonstrated in verse 22? Explain each verse.

14. What do you learn from the attribute that is demonstrated in verse 22?

15. Some authors believe the paralyzed man's malady was caused by his personal sin.

    a. What point in the story indicates that might have been the case?
    b. What are your thoughts about illnesses being a result of personal sin?

16. In verse 23, Jesus says, "Which is easier, to say, 'Your sins are forgiven you,' or to say, 'Rise and walk?'"

    a. What would the problem have been had Jesus simply said, "Your sins are forgiven you"?
    b. What was the point of Jesus telling the man to rise and walk?

17. Luke includes a question in verse 21 asked by the Pharisees, "Who is this who speaks blasphemies?"

    a. How do you define blasphemy?
    b. What does the Bible say about blaspheming the Holy Spirit, and what does that mean?
    c. Is it possible for a true believer to be guilty of blasphemy? Why or why not?

18. In *All the Miracles of the Bible,* Lockyer identifies at least three primary lessons to be gained from the study of this miracle. What lessons can you identify as being taught?[32]

Summary Questions

19. Before accepting Jesus as Savior and Lord, sin runs rampant in people's lives. Answer the following questions:

    a. Once saved, what one or more things happens to the sin that was there before salvation?
    b. Do you have a personal experience you can share?

20. Jesus referred to Himself as the Son of Man in verse 24. This was Jesus's favorite name for Himself, and it is found at least eighty-two times in the Gospel record.

    a. Why do you think that was His favorite name for Himself?
    b. *Challenge.* Why should that name have been so important to the Jewish people? (You may be able to

[32] Lockyer, "The Miracle of the Paralytic," 175–176.

find a reference in the Old Testament that helps with your answer.)

21. What is the most remarkable point about the healing of the paralyzed man?

22. How were the people who witnessed the miracle affected by it?

23. What does the following quote mean to you?

Through Christ's immediate act of intuition, the temper of those scribes was revealed, and all unconsciously they conceded to Him the divine dignity and equality He claimed.[33]

[33] Lockyer, 175.

LESSON 10
Jesus Heals a Man's Withered Hand

Omniscience, omnipotence, and *omnipresence* are three of the attributes of God. He has so many, but these three say so much about Him. The first one, *omniscience* means that He knows all things. That's followed by *omnipotence* which is another way of saying that God is all-powerful. And these three are complete with *omnipresence* which means He is everywhere at all times. It would be hard to rank one over any other since they all work hand in hand to make all things work for good for those who love the Lord.

In the previous lesson, it was obvious that Jesus (God incarnate) was omnipotent. He took a man who had been paralyzed for most of his life—if not all of it—and told him that his sins were forgiven and that he should get up and walk. Can you imagine the look on the man's face, the look on the faces of the men who had taken him to Jesus, and the look of all the faces that witnessed the miracle? To say they were absolutely astonished at this show of omnipotence would be an understatement.

One of the more amazing things about that miracle is that the man who was cured of his malady did not come to Jesus on his own; he was brought to Jesus by four of his friends who had to come in through the roof of the home because the crowd around the Lord was too large to get the paralyzed man through the door. It is not clear whether the man knew Jesus or not, but it is clear that his friends had heard of the healing power of Jesus. This is an example for Christians to heed the calling to bring as many people as possible to experience the spiritual healing that Jesus alone can provide.

The negative aspects of this story, usually present wherever Jesus went, were the naysayers in the persons of Pharisees, Sadducees, Herodians, priests, and scribes. Luke says they had come from every village of Galilee and Judea and from Jerusalem. It was obvious they had not come as followers of the Messiah because they accused Him of blasphemy and asked who could forgive sin other than God. Of course, what they didn't know was that Jesus was God who had come to earth as a man. All the Jewish leaders wanted to do was get evidence to stop the Lord permanently.

What a sad time that was for Israel! Jesus had come first to the biological sons of Abraham so that they could experience the grace that Christ could provide. But they wanted none of that; they wanted to hold on to what they had, and they felt it slipping away. They could have gained that grace by recognizing and trusting in Him as the Messiah, but instead, they walked away angry, having accomplished nothing. How different is that from today? The entire Bible is available to all who want to read it. The church has existed for over 2,000 years. And try as people have, no one has been able to silence the truth of God's Word for all those years. Nonetheless, countless numbers still will not believe what Christ is all about!

However, those who believe in Jesus Christ as Savior and Lord have become the true children of Abraham. That does not mean that all believers are physical descendants of Abraham, but it does mean, much more importantly, that Christians are spiritual descendants. In Galatians 3:7, Paul validated this spiritual connection to Abraham, "Know then that it is those of faith who are the sons of Abraham." Those are very comforting words, particularly since they came from the apostle Paul, the one who was the Jews' Jew and the one who was preaching to the Gentiles. This is the promise made to all people in the first three verses of Genesis 12 when God referred to all the families of the earth.

STUDY GUIDE

Opening Questions

1. Read Mark 2:27–28 and answer the following questions:

    a. What did Jesus mean when He said, "The Sabbath was made for man, not man for the Sabbath"?
    b. What is your opinion of what should or should not be done on Sunday, the Christian Sabbath?
    c. What did Jesus mean when He said, "So the Son of Man is lord even of the Sabbath"?

2. *Challenge.* If you were to be asked who the most important people in the Old Testament were, who would you say they were from the following three groups? Explain your answer.

    a. the patriarchs (narrowly defined consists of Abraham, Isaac, and Jacob)
    b. the kings of Israel who include kings of the unified kingdom, the kings of the southern kingdom after division (Judah), and the kings of the northern kingdom after division (Israel)

c. the prophets (consider seventeen—five major and twelve minor) for whom the books are named

Questions Leading Up to the Performance of the Miracle

3. What story is told right before the performance of the miracle in this lesson? (See Luke 6:1–5.)

4. Why would Jesus have pointed out what and whom He did in these verses from Luke?

5. In Mark 3:1, Mark made this statement, "Again he entered the synagogue." Based on that statement, answer the following two questions:

   a. Why is it important that Mark used the word *again*?
   b. Why is it important to know that Jesus was entering a synagogue of the Jews? (There is both a practical and a spiritual reason.)

Questions about the Miracle

Luke 6:6–11 (also Mark 3:1–6, Matthew 12:9–14)

6. Read Luke 6:6–7 and answer the following questions:

   a. Is there any special significance that verse 6 says it was the man's right hand?

b. What was the sole reason the teachers and Pharisees were paying attention to Jesus, and why were they paying attention to that in particular?
c. What did they expect, and what did they want to do with the expected outcome?
d. What does that tell you about those two groups of people (teachers, Pharisees)?

7. From the verses for this miracle, how is it known that the scribes and the Pharisees did not have a chance against Jesus?

8. Depending on what you found in question 7 above, can you provide one or more other verses where the people challenging Jesus could not possibly have won an argument?

9. There are two things curious about this miracle: (a) The man did not have a life-threatening condition, and (b) Jesus could have postponed the healing until the next day. Therefore, why didn't he delay so that a conflict about the Sabbath would not be stirred up in the synagogue? There can be more than one answer to this question.

10. Read the account of the same miracle in Mark 3:1–6. What is so evil and ironic in verses 5 and 6?

11. There are as many as four teachings that come from this miracle. Review the miracle and then see what teachings you can identify.

Summary Questions

12. After reading both Luke's and Mark's recordings of the miracle, express your thoughts about how Jesus felt about the scribes and Pharisees at this time.

13. How did this miracle affect the following:

    a. the one who performed the miracle
    b. the one on whom the miracle was performed
    c. the ones who witnessed the miracle

14. Is there anything in the statement below that is particularly significant to you? Does anything convict, encourage, or enrich you?

One of the resources used for this lesson, Lockyer's *All the Miracles of the Bible*, recommends reading "Jesus Angry with Hard Hearts," a sermon by Charles Spurgeon. It is a long sermon, but something fascinating is said near the very start of it, "A poor man was present in the synagogue ... (and in) the same synagogue was the Saviour, ready to restore to that hand all its wonted force and cunning. Happy conjunction!"[34] Isn't that just like Jesus? He's ready to heal when anyone is ready to be healed!

---

[34] Lockyer, "The Miracle of the Withered Hand," 177.

LESSON 11
Jesus Raises a Boy from the Dead

The first five miracles were reviewed in Lesson 7, and this is always good practice with any study. The following four miracles, reviewed here, have been studied since that initial review of the first five.

1. *Jesus Healed a Leper.* The leper knew whose presence he was in because he fell to his knees (or fell on his face) when he approached the Lord. The man knew that Jesus could heal him if He would choose to, showing both faith and doubt. Jesus had the power to heal, and He chose to do that for the leper.

2. *Jesus Healed the Centurion's Servant.* Jews were the chosen people of God, yet the centurion, a Gentile, had more faith than anyone in Israel. What did *that* show? Most importantly, and what the Jewish leadership did not realize, was that Jesus had come to be the Savior of all who accepted Him as the Messiah. Jesus's offering of salvation to Jews and Gentiles was one of the reasons He fell into such disfavor with the Jewish hierarchy.

3. *Jesus Healed a Paralyzed Man.* Can one affect the eternal life of another? Did the four friends of this paralyzed man affect the eternal life of their friend? The answer is yes to both questions

as demonstrated by this miracle. Leading others to have eternal life through Jesus is what is expected of all Christians.

4. *Jesus Healed a Withered Hand.* The man was not facing a life-threatening illness, but Jesus chose to heal him on the Sabbath and in the synagogue. The Jewish leaders were outraged that Jesus would do this type of work on the Sabbath (heal a human), yet these leaders would have gladly pulled their donkey out of a ditch on the Sabbath (save an animal). This shows how hypocritical the Jewish hierarchy was.

What lessons can be learned from studying these first nine miracles? There are many, but the following are some of the more important ones:

- Jesus was to be about His Father's work, and so are His followers today;
- A person never knows whose life might be touched when Jesus is shared;
- Evil caused the possessed man to be tormented; Jesus healed the man then as He heals us today;
- A believer's role is to *get up* and serve the Lord whenever and wherever he or she is;
- Jesus may tell a follower to do something contrary to their thoughts; however, just do it;
- Not only can Jesus heal a malady, but He does if it is what He chooses to do;
- Jesus was for the Jews and the Gentiles then just as He is now;

- Bring another to Jesus, and then let Jesus work His miracles on that person's life; and
- Love is the key by which Jesus operated; it should be the same for Christians today.

Nine miracles from the Bible have been studied so far with many more to come, and there have been nine great lessons for the believer. Jesus affected the lives of the people when He performed these miraculous acts, and He can affect lives similarly today when the lessons He taught are put into action. It's not always easy, but with prayer and the leading of the Holy Spirit, all followers of Jesus can come closer to how He wants his followers to live.

STUDY GUIDE

Opening Questions

5. The text for this miracle will refer to the *gate of the town*. While that would certainly serve as an entry point into the town, why was a gate so important for people during Jesus's time?

6. Although there are several *resurrections from the dead* in the Bible, there are only three resurrections from the dead recorded that Jesus performed. Not counting the raising of the dead of the widow's son in this lesson's miracle, who were the other two? Give a little information on each.

7. See if you can find any notable resurrections of the dead in the Old Testament and in the New Testament after the resurrection and ascension of Jesus. Give a little information about each.

8. One of the attributes of God is providence or divine providence. Provide a definition of providence.

9. How does providence compare to coincidence? Should a Christian believe in coincidence? Why or why not?

Questions Leading Up to the Performance of the Miracle

It was the day after Jesus had been working a wondrous miracle in the healing of the centurion's servant. Full of blessing, full of life, full of salvation, and full of healing, He went His way, and wherever He went, something happened to mark Him who was more than an ordinary man and was walking through the cities and the villages of Palestine.[35]

10. After reading the quote above, share when you most see Jesus as full of blessing, life, salvation, and healing. This can be from a Bible story or from something in your life.

11. What is the difference between a bier and a coffin?

[35] Mary Elizabeth Baxter, "Widow of Nain," accessed March 1, 2019, https://www.blueletterbible.org/Comm/baxter_mary/WitW/WitW36_WidowOfNain.cfm.

Questions about the Miracle

Luke 7:11–17

12. Luke 7:11 begins with this statement, "Soon afterward he went to a town called Nain." To what is "soon afterward" referring? That is, soon after what?

13. Jesus departed Capernaum and went to the town of Nain. What can you find out about this town? What is the meaning of the word *Nain*? Where was this town located in comparison to other notable towns and villages in Israel of Jesus's time? What other additional facts can you discover?

14. As Jesus arrived in the town, two crowds of people met.

    a. Who were the two crowds?
    b. Explain the similarities and differences between the two crowds.
    c. What might this meeting of the two crowds symbolize in the faith of believers?

15. How does divine providence play into this miracle?

16. Luke says in verse 12, "A man who had died was being carried out, the only son of his mother, and she was a widow." What makes this statement so important to the understanding of this miracle?

17. *Challenge.* To understand God's provision for everyone, find one or more references from the Old Testament that demonstrate how the less fortunate (widows, orphans, sojourners, etc.) were to be taken care of by those who were more fortunate.

18. What meaning or meanings can be taken from the fact that so many people attended the funeral and the burial of the widow's son?

19. Which one of the following explains the action Jesus took with the widow's son? Explain your answer.

    a. Jesus was offering credentials for His ministry.
    b. Jesus was attempting to silence His critics by showing who He was.
    c. Jesus was demonstrating His infinite sympathy for human suffering.

20. Luke 7:14 states, "Then he came up and touched the bier, and the bearers stood still." Answer the following questions regarding that statement.

    a. What would the Pharisees have found negative about what Jesus did, and what effect would that have had on Jesus's credibility in their minds?
    b. Why was the action of Jesus so important to those who witnessed it?
    c. What do you think the "bearers stood still" means?

21. What can you assume about Jesus from His words at the end of verse 14, "Young man, I say to you, arise"?

22. After Jesus spoke those words in verse 14, "And the dead man sat up and began to speak." While one can't know for sure, what might he have been saying?

23. Early in the miracle Jesus is referred to as *he,* yet later Jesus is referred to as *Lord.* Why might using the different terms for Jesus be so important in Luke's telling of this miracle?

Summary Questions

24. Other people in the scripture raised the dead to life, but there is a major difference between those people raising the dead and Jesus doing so. What is that major difference?

25. How did this miracle affect those who witnessed it?

26. How did this miracle affect those who had become enemies of the Lord?

27. What is similar in this lesson's miracle and 1 Thessalonians 4:13–18?

28. Why is it so important to the understanding of this miracle to note that no one asked Jesus to perform it?

29. Is there anything in the quote below that is particularly important or intriguing to you? Why?

Why should it be thought a thing incredible that God should raise the dead? If He is supreme in the universe, then it is easy to believe in resurrection, however stupendous the miracle may be. Surely, He who created man from dust is able to call him forth again from the domain of death, if He should so please. As the Life, He was (is) also the Resurrection.[36]

---

[36] Lockyer, "The Miracle of the Widow's Son," 181.

LESSON 12
Jesus Calms the Storm

The man in Lesson 10 had a withered hand; that's bad enough in and of itself. Notably, the withered hand was his right hand. Since a considerable proportion, perhaps 90 percent, of the population is right-handed, it is to be assumed that the man in the miracle was right-handed. That meant that not only did he have a withered hand, but it also meant that the withered hand was the one that he would have worked with. Therefore, in a manual society such as the one Jesus came to, this disability would have meant the man could not do much work to earn a living. But there is more to this than might appear on the surface.

The right hand, both in Jesus's time and probably to a lesser extent today, symbolized the opposite of wrong, something that conforms to a particular standard and to a place of honor or authority. When you investigate these words in the Bible, you begin to realize the importance of the right hand. When Jacob blessed Joseph's sons, the son sitting to his right was given greater honor. At the final judgment, the sheep (those saved) will go to the right, and the goats (those lost) will go to the left. After Christ died on the cross, rose from the dead, and ascended to the Father, He was placed at the right hand of God. There are many more uses of the right hand in the Bible, but the three given above are some of the more memorable ones.

It is interesting how Jesus in this miracle saw a man with a need and not a needy man. What is the difference? There is something a man with a need is lacking, and a simple or miraculous happening is all that is required to satisfy the need. The man in the miracle had probably worked in the past, and he wanted to do that again. On the other hand, a needy man is more likely to be one without means who may not necessarily be willing to work to satisfy what he needs.

From a spiritual standpoint, what was Jesus teaching? He wanted people to understand that all mankind has a need whether or not they recognize it. A needy man must be saved from the penalty of sin so that he can live forever in paradise with the Lord. Until it is recognized that one's spirit is withered and needs to be renewed or restored, work for the kingdom will not be done, and the greatest promise and gift given to man will not be attained. This is how every miracle should be understood.

No matter what the miracle—turning water to wine, raising the widow's son, or any of the other miracles—there is a spiritual message that goes along with the physical one. While Jesus was on earth and was working His miracles, there was joy in His heart that He could heal someone and restore them to life or health or happiness. But a student of Jesus's miracles must also understand that every one of the teachings of Jesus was meant to draw people close to Him, to accept the grace that God offers, and to look forward to life eternal with Him. What more could be desired than that?

In this lesson's study, stay alert to what the spiritual message might be. Without paying attention to that, you likely will miss the entire point of the story Jesus was teaching with His physical actions. That is not just a lesson for Jesus's time. When anything happens in life, the Christian should always look for what Jesus wants to be known and understood. Until a person can do that, he is missing what the Lord wants to show. When people can do that, they will be drawn closer and closer to Christ so that the peace of Christ will become more and more evident in all they do. How joyous do you think the man healed of the withered hand was? Christians can be just that joyful!

STUDY GUIDE

Opening Questions

1. In some of Jesus's miracles, the reader is told that He *rebuked* something—fever, frenzy of the demoniac, a tempest. Authors of the Bible could have said *got rid of, eliminated, disposed of,* or some other word instead of *rebuked.* Why do you think the authors chose the word *rebuked*?

2. Read John 16:33 along with Deuteronomy 31:8. What two promises can the Christian be assured of based on God's Holy Word?

3. How well do you personally use the promise from Deuteronomy to deal with the promise of John 16:33?

Questions Leading Up to the Performance of the Miracle

4. Scan Mark 4:1–34. Make a list of the various activities Jesus had been doing just prior to the performance of the miracle in this lesson.

5. In the first verse of the Scripture for this miracle, Mark 4:35, Jesus said, "Let us go across to the other side." What is meant by *the other side*, and why is this significant to understanding the events that take place? (Do you see God's providence at work here?)

6. Verse 36 says "They took him with them in the boat, just as he was." Why do you think Mark chose to use the words *just as he was*?

Questions about the Miracle

Mark 4:35–41 (also Matthew 8:23–27, Luke 8:22–25, John 6:16–21)

7. Jesus went with *them* in the boat, but the verses do not indicate who *them* were.

    a. Who might one or more of *them* have been?
    b. Why can that assumption be made?

8. Read the first sentence of verse 38. How is it that Jesus could have been asleep? Use Proverbs 3:24, Psalm 4:8, and any other Bible verses to explain Jesus's calmness.

9. Read the second sentence of verse 38 and then answer the following questions:

    a. What is positive about what the disciples did in this verse?
    b. What is negative about their actions?
    c. How can you relate personally to both sides of what the disciples did?
    d. What can you do to have your actions become more like the positive actions of the disciples?

10. How would you compare the faith of the centurion in a previous miracle to the faith of the disciples in this lesson?

11. Tell what you think each of the following words from this miracle symbolizes in our lives and in our faith:

    a. the sea
    b. the wind
    c. the boat

12. Read Jonah 1:4–6 along with the scripture for this lesson. What do you see as major differences between the two stories of a tempest on the sea? (There may be three or more differences.)

Summary Questions

13. It is always a good idea to look at a Bible story from the various writers' points of view. Go back, read, and compare this miracle in all four of the Gospels (Mark 4:35–41, Matthew 8:23–27, Luke 8:22–25, John 6:16–21). Is there anything added, left out, or stated differently in these four accounts?

14. In what one or more ways does this miracle show the human side of Jesus and the divine side of Jesus?

15. Keeping the previous question in mind, why is it so important that the human side of the Messiah is remembered? Give biblical support for your answer if you can.

16. How did this miracle affect the one who performed the miracle?

17. How did this miracle affect those for whom the miracle was performed?

18. Based on this miracle, what comfort is offered to all believers?

19. What was most convicting for you about this miracle?

LESSON 13
Jesus Casts Demons into a Pig Herd

The following reference may seem irreverent at first, but hopefully, it will be seen as having relevance to what will be studied in this lesson. If you consider it irreverent or inappropriate, it is certainly not intended that way.

One of the great comic philosophers in the early to mid-1970s was Flip Wilson, and he was most famous for creating two characters—Geraldine (Wilson in drag) and Reverend Leroy who was the minister of the Church of What's Happening Now. "New parishioners were wary of coming to the church as it was hinted that Reverend Leroy was a con artist. Wilson popularized the catchphrase 'The Devil made me do it.'" The reverend used this phrase whenever he was caught in a sin, and Geraldine even used a version of it when she would say, "The devil made me buy this dress!" Both quotes are examples of people who did not take responsibility for what they did in their lives (Flip Wilson, *Wikipedia*).

Getting back to the more serious study of God's Word, however, the blame that Wilson made popular in his comedy routine is seen replete throughout the scriptures, and there is a very short wait to see the first occurrence. Additionally, in the present world, this same philosophy is alive and well today—in schools, in government, in sports, in everyday lives, and even in churches. In other words, the game of blaming others for what happens runs rampant.

Consider the third chapter of Genesis, the chapter in which Adam and Eve were tempted by the devil, succumbed to his temptations, and committed the first sin known to man—disobeying what God had told them to do and not to do. After a bit of dialog with Adam, God asked him, "'Have you eaten of the tree of which I commanded you not to eat?' The man said, 'The woman whom you gave to be with me, she gave me fruit of the tree, and I ate.' The Lord God said to the woman, 'What is this that you have done?' The woman said, 'The serpent deceived me, and I ate.'" Did the devil make them do it? Were Adam and Eve involved in choosing their sin? Did the man and woman act of their own volition?

Perhaps another question needs to be asked, "Is God part of any *conspiracy* that leads people to do things that are against His commands, laws, and expectations?" No. This is a question that has baffled men for centuries and will probably continue to do so until men begin to accept the Word of God as the true and pure words of the Lord.

In the book that bears his name, James, the half-brother of Jesus, said, "Let no one say when he is tempted, 'I am being tempted by God,' for God cannot be tempted with evil, and himself tempts no one" (James 1:13). Earlier in the same chapter, James wrote, "Count it all joy, my brothers, when you meet trials of various kinds, for you know that the testing of your faith produces steadfastness. And let steadfastness have its full effect, that you may be perfect and complete, lacking in nothing" (James 1:2–4).

God will not tempt people thus leading them to sin, but He may well allow people to be tempted to have challenges presented to a person to see if they can meet those challenges in the way Christ would have them met. When that is done, mankind has done what Jesus wants His children to do, and His children will grow stronger in Christ Jesus, the believer's Savior and Lord.

STUDY GUIDE

Opening Questions

1. *Challenge.* There are ways the devil's power is exercised (a) directly by himself, (b) through demons who are subject to the devil, and (c) through humans who are influenced by the devil. See if you can find a Bible passage that reflects each of those. Give book, chapter, and verse(s) to support your answer.

2. Since this lesson focuses on demons or unclean spirits, give a biblical definition for either or both of those terms. You may want to use a Bible dictionary for your answers.

Questions Leading Up to the Performance of the Miracle

3. Since *immediately* was a word often used by Mark, how many times did he use it in his Gospel, and more importantly, why would he have chosen to use that word so often?

4. Matthew mentioned demoniacs (Matthew 8:28) while Mark 5:2 and Luke 8:27 refer to a single demoniac. Does this represent an inconsistency in scripture? Explain your answer whether it is yes or no.

Questions about the Miracle

Mark 5:1–20 (also Matthew 8:28–33, Luke 8:26–39)

5. Based on all the verses for this miracle, can you find anything that would lead you to believe that the people living in this area were primarily Gentiles or Jews?

6. The very first line of the scripture for this lesson says, "They came to the other side of the sea, to the country of the Gerasenes." (King James Version [KJV] says "Gadarenes," and there may be other names as well.)

    a. To whom does the word *they* refer?
    b. Where was "the other side of the sea"?
    c. What happened *immediately* (one of Mark's favorite words) when Jesus stepped out of the boat?

7. Give a description of the demoniac based on verses 2–5.

8. Parts of verses 6 and 7 say, "When he saw Jesus from afar, he ran and fell down before him" and "What have you to do with me?"

    a. Who is speaking in each of those statements?
    b. Why is there such a change between the first statement and the second?

9. Mark 5:7 says, "What have you to do with me, Jesus, Son of the Most-High God?" while Matthew 8:29 says, "What have you to do with us, O Son of God? *Have you come to torment us before the time?*" What did Matthew mean with the italicized sentence?

10. Depending on the version of the Bible you use, you may see the word *adjure* in verse 7.

    a. What does the word mean?
    b. Why was it used by the speaker in this instance?
    c. What does it tell you about Jesus and demons?

11. Jesus asked the man his name, and the man answered, "My name is Legion, for we are many." Why did Jesus ask his name, and what is the deeper meaning behind the name Legion?

12. Jesus could have done anything He wanted to do with the demons, but He chose to send them into a herd of pigs. Come up with one or more reasons why He chose to do what He did with the demons. Would the owners of the pigs being (a) Jews or (b) Gentiles change your answer? How?

13. What action did the following take, and why did they do what they did? What do their actions say about each of them?

    a. the swineherds (keepers of the pigs)
    b. the people who wanted Jesus to depart from the region

14. Identify the requests made of Jesus in Mark 5:12–20 and explain how and why Jesus responded to each of the requests.

15. As a believer, what message or messages do you receive for yourself personally regarding what Jesus said to the man who had been cleansed of the demon?

Summary Questions

16. One commentary says that there were three forces at work in this miracle.

    a. What are those three forces?
    b. Explain the effectiveness of each, listing the order of effectiveness of each of them (least effective to most) and why you listed them in the order you did.

17. *Challenge.* Verse 20 refers to the Decapolis.

    a. What was the Decapolis?
    b. Where was the Decapolis?
    c. What message was Jesus sending by being in the Decapolis—both for people of His time on earth and for us today?

18. How did this miracle affect the one who performed it?

19. How did this miracle affect the one on whom it was performed?

20. How did this miracle affect the ones who witnessed it?

21. What thoughts do you have after reading the statement below?

As Christians, we can take comfort in the knowledge that the forces of the enemy of our souls are under the complete control of God and can only act in ways He allows.[37]

[37] "Why did Jesus allow the demons to enter the herd of pigs?," https://www.gotquestions.org/jesus-demons-pigs.html.

LESSON 14
Jesus Heals a Woman with Blood Issues

People may have multiple priorities with each of them being important for different reasons. This can take a toll on the person. Some people can handle various activities and priorities at a high level. Christians who succeed in multi-tasking (1) believe God has led them to each activity, (2) are willing and able to use God's gifts because He has given them the ability, and (3) believe that prayer before undertaking any activity is the first step in any process. You may know people just like that, and you wonder, "How can one person do so many things so well?"

Although the person described above is human, stop and think about what the master of multitasking did while He was on earth. He was a

- Preacher: His Sermon on the Mount is the greatest sermon of all time;
- Teacher: He taught many, and He taught His disciples to take over when He left;
- Leader: He led and got the best from a motley crew of twelve not particularly gifted men;

- Manager: He managed squabbles and complaints by making decisions;
- Critic: He was willing to criticize those who did not want to know the truth about God;
- Straight-shooter: He never backed down with the truth His Father had given Him;
- Caregiver: He loved those whom He met with unmatched compassion;
- Miracle worker: He cured all who came to Him no matter what malady they had, and
- Promise keeper: He never went back on His word to God or to man.

While the list is remarkable, it was not uncommon for Him to be many of these things at once. He might preach to the crowds in a way that taught His disciples and, at the same time criticize those who were at odds with the truth, shooting straight with them while caring for them. The Bible only gives a snapshot of His accomplishments in the three years He ministered to the masses. John, the disciple He loved, stated, "Now there are also many other things that Jesus did. Were every one of them to be written, I suppose that the world itself could not contain the books that would be written" (John 21:25).

Before getting started with this lesson, read what Herbert Lockyer says in his book *All the Miracles of Jesus*, "The miracle we are now to consider was a miracle sandwiched in between two halves of another miracle ... We can call this one a parenthesis miracle." This is like an Oreo cookie with the dark brown wafers on the outside being the "before and the after" miracle and the white filling being the "actual miracle."

When there are two or more things of importance going on in a person's life, that person may find themselves in varying degrees of confusion, panic, anxiety, and/or concern. Yet in the miracle that followed, Jesus focused on taking one action when another action interfered. But these are not the types of problems ordinary people might face; they are issues of physical life on the one hand and of physical healing on the other. Jesus knew what was at stake, and He also knew that He had this. He delayed going to a dying daughter to take care of the woman with a life-defeating illness. In the end, one was given freedom from her condition, and the other was given freedom from the grave. That is the kind of multitasking Jesus did, and He continues to work like that, through the Holy Spirit, in our lives today. It is so comforting to know that He can do more than one thing at a time!

STUDY GUIDE

Opening Questions

1. The crowds were very different at the close of the previous miracle (demon sent into pigs) and the opening of this miracle.
    a. What was the difference in the two crowds?
    b. What would Jesus have found appealing about both crowds?
    c. What do His actions tell about the responsibilities of Christians today?
2. What are the main reasons you see Jesus going into both Gentile areas and Jewish areas?

3. Once Christ ascended, the Holy Spirit came, and the New Testament church was up and running, who was charged with ministry to the Gentiles and to the Jews and why?

Questions Leading Up to the Performance of the Miracle

Mark 5:21–24

4. What was the role of a ruler of the synagogue?

5. What made this particular man different with regard to many of the Jewish leaders of Jesus's day?

Questions about the Miracle

Mark 5:25–34 (also Matthew 9:20–22, Luke 8:43–48)

6. If you look at Matthew, Mark, and Luke where the miracle is recorded, what is one significant difference found in Matthew from what is in Mark and Luke? See what you can find out about why this difference may have occurred.

7. What does Luke tell us about the disease of the woman that Mark does not?

8. There were at least two negative consequences, possibly more, for the condition that had maligned this woman for so many years. Give two or more of these consequences (don't include the fact that she had spent all her money on a cure).

9. Looking at the money side of the story, what might some of the consequences have been because she had spent all her money on cures?

10. Answer the following questions about Jesus and the woman.

    a. Can you assume the woman had seen Jesus before? Why or why not?
    b. Based on your answer to the question above, what one or more things are said about the woman?
    c. Again, based on your first answer, what does that say about Jesus?

11. E. R. Micklem in his book *Miracles and the New Psychology* says, "To her, in her desperate need, necessity knew no law."[38] Based on verse 27, what did Micklem mean with his statement? Find an Old Testament reference that speaks to this law.

12. Read verse 29 and explain how the information in that verse goes along with a fact associated with many of the other miracles of Jesus. What does that say about Jesus?

13. What does it mean that "power had gone out from him" (Jesus)? Specifically, does that mean that Christ had lost some of His power? Whether yes or no, explain your answer.

14. *Challenge.* Concerning the power having gone out of Jesus, *The Bible Knowledge Commentary* says, "One view maintains that God the Father healed the woman and Jesus was not aware of it

---

[38] E. R. Micklem, "Woman with a Haemorrhage," *Miracles and the New Psychology* (London: Oxford University Press, 1922), 120–123.

till afterward. The other view is that Jesus Himself, wishing to honor the woman's faith, willingly extended His healing power to her."[39] Which of those do you agree with and why?

15. Knowing what Jesus was like during His ministry on earth, why do you think He would have wanted to know who had touched Him?

16. Answer the following questions regarding the woman:

    a. Why would she have come "in fear and trembling"?
    b. Why did she feel the need to tell the "whole truth"?

17. Matthew Henry states the following in his commentary, "Many of his messages and some of his miracles, are recorded as taking place while he walked along the road to somewhere; we should be doing good not only when we sit in the house but also when we walk by the way."[40] Using this statement and Deuteronomy 6:7, give your thoughts on the following two questions.

    a. What did the verse from Deuteronomy mean to Jesus?
    b. What should the statement by Matthew Henry and the verse from Deuteronomy mean for believers?

---

[39] John F. Walvoord and Roy B. Zuck, "The Healing of the Woman with a Hemorrhage," in *The Bible Knowledge Commentary* (Wheaton: Victor Books, 1983), 125.

[40] Matthew Henry, "Mark 5:21–34," in *The New Matthew Henry Commentary* (Grand Rapids: Zondervan, 2010),1578.

Summary Questions

18. Jesus healed a leper in Mark 1, and in verse 44 of that chapter, He told the leper, "See that you say nothing to anyone." However, in this lesson, Jesus asked in Mark 5:30, "Who touched my garments?" In the first instance, Jesus wanted nothing said about the miracle, but in the second instance Jesus stopped everyone and everything to find out who had touched Him thus bringing the miracle to the attention of everyone.

    a. Why do you think Jesus responded differently in the two miracles?
    b. In his book *All the Miracles of the Bible,* Lockyer sees one or more positive aspects of the woman's faith and one or more negative aspects of the woman's faith.[41] Give one or more positive aspects of her faith and give one or more negative aspects of her faith.

19. How did the miracle affect the one who performed it?

20. How did the miracle affect the one on whom the miracle was performed?

21. How did the miracle affect the disciples?

22. Read the information below. Explain how the sentence from a sermon and the scripture passage below go together.

In Mark 5:31 Jesus asked who had touched Him. His disciples, seemingly indignant said, "You see the crowd pressing around

[41] Lockyer, "The Miracle of the Woman with an Issue of Blood," 194–197.

you, and yet you say, 'Who touched me?'" The following statement was made in a sermon titled "Our feelings do not affect God's facts!" The disciples *felt* it was impossible for Jesus to find out who touched Him while Jesus continued to pursue a *fact.* This is another example of where it would be good for all believers to go back and read Isaiah 55:8–9!

LESSON 15
Jesus Raises Jairus's Daughter from the Dead

There were lots of different groups of players in the time of Jesus, and a number of them were those who did not like Jesus even a little bit. Of course, there were some in each of the groups that were inclined to believe differently than the majority, and those were the ones who really had nerves of steel to take a minority stand. Look at just a few comments about each of the groups to get a better idea of what Jesus faced.

Pharisees. Meaning separated in Aramaic, this was a group that held to the immortality of the soul, the resurrection of the dead, and punishment in future life based upon how one lived in this life. The wicked would be imprisoned forever under the earth, but those who were righteous would live again. They were more concerned with outward appearance than inward feelings, and they added a tremendous amount of traditional material that was passed from generation to generation. Of all the groups in the Jewish faith, they were the most conservative, they came from more of the blue-collar class, and they were the most obvious persecutors of the Lord.

Sadducees. The Sadducees were a Jewish political party, were members of the priesthood, and were part of the Sanhedrin (see below). High priests were chosen from the Sadducees, were educated, and were usually wealthy. According to Acts 23, they did not believe in resurrection, angels, or spirits. They were in opposition to the Pharisees, but to rid themselves of Jesus, they banded together with the Pharisees when it was helpful for them to reach their own goals.

Sanhedrin. The name comes from a combination of two Greek words that mean seated together. The Sanhedrin consisted of seventy members with the high priest as the chief officer for a total of seventy-one. This number was most likely patterned after the seventy men who were chosen to assist Moses in solving disputes among the Israelites while they were wandering in the desert. The Gospels call them the council of the elders, and they ruled under the Romans in civil and religious matters. When the city of Jerusalem was destroyed in AD 70, the Sanhedrin was abolished since Jerusalem was no longer theirs.

Herodians. Even though they were Jewish, they were a political party that wanted to restore the Herodian dynasty to the throne in Judea and in other areas previously ruled by Herod the Great. Because of this desire, they were political foes of the Pharisees who wished to restore the kingdom of David. Rarely mentioned (only three times in the Gospels), any reference to them was always in conjunction with the Pharisees. After Jesus challenged their interpretation of the Sabbath, they plotted to kill Him and aligned themselves with the Pharisees.

Scribes. The Greek word for scribe means writer; they were the ones in the Jewish hierarchy who drew up legal documents and copied the Old Testament scriptures. In addition, they studied the law to determine daily life applications for it. Noted scribes had their own disciples because they studied the scriptures with respect to doctrinal and historical matters. Many of the scribes were members of the Jewish council. Most of them were opposed to Jesus and were in large part responsible for His death. Later, they were involved in the persecutions of Peter and John and were involved in the martyrdom of Stephen.

Elders. Elders of the people of Israel were older men who represented the people and who exercised a certain amount of authority over them. The elders would play a big part in causing the suffering and death of Jesus (Matthew 16:21, Mark 8:31, Luke 9:22) and along with chief priests and scribes, challenged Jesus's authority just days before the crucifixion. The elders and chief priests were the ones who bribed Judas to betray Jesus, and they were among the groups of leaders assembled at the High Priest's palace just before the New Testament Passover. As if that were not enough, the elders were partly responsible for getting the people to request the release of Barabbas and were some of those who mocked Jesus on the cross.

Priests. The high priest was taken from the Sadducees, and two of them, Annas and Caiaphas, father-in-law and son-in-law, figured prominently in the death of Jesus. Annas was the high priest from AD 6 to AD 15 but was removed from the office by the Romans. Nonetheless, he continued to wield considerable power behind the scenes. Caiaphas was the high priest at the time of Jesus's ministry. Both were extremely powerful people in the Jewish hierarchy.

Rulers of the Synagogue. The ruler of the synagogue was the administrative official with the duty of preserving order and inviting persons to read or speak in the assembly. Further, he examined the discourses of the public speakers and saw that all things were done with decency and in accordance with ancestral usage. Jairus was a ruler of the synagogue, and at least two others are mentioned by the names Crispus and Sosthenes. Acts 18:8 states that Crispus and all his house believed in the Lord, and the other one, Sosthenes, also a believer, was beaten before the judgment seat by Greeks in Acts 18:17.

Essenes. Different from other groups at the time of Jesus, the Essenes were a shadowy group who lived alongside the Dead Sea. Although not mentioned directly in the New Testament, there are a couple of passages that may refer to them: Luke 22:10–12 and Acts 6:7. Little is known about them, and most of what is known has been provided by Josephus and Philo in their writings. On another note, there have been buildings discovered next to the Dead Sea, and it has been argued that these buildings are where the Essenes lived. It is also assumed that the Dead Sea Scrolls were placed in caves in the general area where the Essenes may have lived.

Although not exhaustive, the groups listed above were very prominent players in what took place during the time Jesus was on earth—with the exception of the Essenes. It is important to know and understand the Pharisees, the Sadducees, the priests, the scribes, the elders, the Herodians, and the Sanhedrin. All of these had important roles in the abuse of Jesus and in the acts and trials that took place which led to His death on the cross.

STUDY GUIDE

One crowd sighed with relief as they saw Jesus leave, but another crowd was waiting to welcome Him when He returned home to Capernaum. In that latter crowd stood two people who were especially anxious to see Him—Jairus, a man with a dying daughter, and an anonymous woman suffering from an incurable disease. It was Jairus who approached Jesus first, but it was the woman who was first helped.[42]

Opening Questions

1. Read the quote above. Today where can one see a group sigh with relief when they see Jesus leave and another group welcome Him into their midst? (There is no one particular answer.)

2. What message or messages do you get from the fact that Jesus stopped His visit to Jairus's home and took time to heal the woman with the bleeding issue (Lesson 14)?

3. What do you think would have been Jairus's reaction to this?

Questions Leading Up to the Performance of the Miracle

Mark 5:21–24

4. Regarding some of the Jewish leaders, answer the following questions:

    a. What would they have thought of Jairus taking the action he took? Why?
    b. Why would Jairus have taken the action he did regardless of what the leaders thought?

5. See what you can find out about the name Jairus.

---

[42] Wiersbe, "Victory Over Disease," 103, https://www.logos.com.

6. What comparisons or contrasts can be assumed about Jairus and the bleeding woman?

7. Verse 23 in the *ESV* begins "and implored him earnestly." Read several different versions of the Bible and see what different words are used. Which set of words gets the point across more strongly to you than others? Why?

8. Compare Jairus's level of faith to the Centurion's level of faith (Lesson 8 "Jesus Heals the Centurion's Servant"). Should the levels of faith have been just the opposite? Why or why not?

Questions about the Miracle

Mark 5:35–43 (also Matthew 9:18–26, Luke 8:41–56)

9. What point were those who spoke to Jairus in verse 35 really making, particularly about Jesus?

10. Read verse 36 and then answer the following:

    a. What do you think Jesus's unsaid message was to those reporting the daughter was dead?
    b. Jesus said, "Do not fear, only believe." What do you think He was really saying to Jairus?
    c. Why do you think Jesus did not simply tell Jairus that his daughter would be okay?

11. Even though the message had been received that the daughter was dead, Jesus went on to the home of Jairus. When they got

there, "Jesus saw a commotion, people weeping and wailing loudly."

a. Who do you think were the people wailing loudly? Why?
b. What did those actions say about the little girl's status?

12. What did Jesus mean when He said, "This child is not dead but sleeping"?

13. What reaction did the people have, and what might this have revealed about this particular crowd and its knowledge of or experience with Jesus?

14. Jesus went into where the child was and took "the child's father and mother and those who were with Him."

a. Complete the whole list of those who were with Jesus.
b. As they went into the room where the girl was, explain why Jesus limited the number of individuals who went in with Him.

15. What two instructions did Jesus give to the parents? Why would He have done that?

Summary Questions

16. One resource, Adam Clarke, a British Methodist theologian in the eighteenth and nineteenth centuries, noticed that four things displayed by Jairus are necessary for answered prayer. Based on this miracle, what might those four things be? Your list may agree with Clarke's or it may be different.

17. *Challenge.* An unusual word, *soul-sleep,* was used in some comments in relation to this miracle. Answer the following questions about this word.

    a. What does soul-sleep mean?
    b. Does mainstream Christianity believe in soul-sleep. Why or why not?

18. See what one or more things you can find that are similar in (a) Jesus raising the widow of Nain's son, (b) Jesus raising the daughter of Jairus, and (c) Jesus raising Lazarus. The first two have been covered in this study, but the last one has not. Depending on what you find that is similar, what does that say about Jesus?

19. How were the various people mentioned in the story affected by this miracle?

20. In relation to various other comments Jesus made about faith, what do you think of the statement below?

Jesus did not demand that Jairus show the same faith as the centurion had. Jesus responded to the faith Jairus had, and He asks us to give Him the faith that we have.[43]

---

[43] David Guzik, "Study Guide for Luke 8," https://www.blueletterbible.org/comm/guzik_david/study-guide/luke/luke-8.cfm.

LESSON 16
Jesus Heals Two Blind Men

In a span of a very short period of time, this study of the miracles has covered Jesus raising a widow's son from the dead, calming the sea, ridding either one or two men from the ravages of evil spirits living in them, curing a woman of a bleeding disease that had lasted for twelve years, and raising back to life the daughter of one of the synagogue officials. While that might seem like a good day's work, it can be assumed that was not all that He did. Why can that be assumed? It was because John in his Gospel said, "Jesus also did many other things. If they were all written down, I suppose the entire world could not contain the books that would be written" (John 21:25). Subsequently, there is no record about what else He may have done during this brief period of time.

Sometimes people who do not believe as Christians, and even some of those who claim to be Christians, question the authenticity of the miracles that God has brought about in the world. Although they may not say that this or that event did not occur, they may say that there is a better way to explain what might have happened. Reflecting on a few of the more phenomenal miraculous events will show what man can do to distort what God has done.

The creation. While people have argued since time began

whether the universe and all that is in it was created over billions of years or in six twenty-four-hour days, it is a travesty to argue that there was a single molecule that evolved into everything that has ever been created. If there is a God, they say, He may have gotten the ball rolling, but evolution took care of the rest.

The parting of the Red Sea. Christians believe God miraculously parted the Red Sea while the Israelites crossed over, and He then let the waters flow together again to kill the Egyptians who were in pursuit of them. There are those, of course, who would prefer to look at some freak of nature as being the reason the sea parted such as a hot desert wind or a windstorm could have done what Christians know God did.

The resurrection of our Lord. Imagine this absurd scenario, Jesus did not really die but was still alive when they took Him down from the cross! He was then taken to a secret place to be resuscitated, so He could be raised from the dead. If that is true, then there is no meaning for the Christian faith, but because it is true, Christians have salvation founded on His dying to forgive sins and His resurrection to give eternal life. The apostle Paul said that if there was no resurrection, Christians are the people who should be most pitied for what they believe (1 Corinthians 15:19).

If Jesus had performed His miracles in secret where no one else witnessed them, then perhaps He could be called a charlatan who was trying to get away with something. However, Jesus raised the widow's son in the presence of two big crowds of people. He calmed the sea in the presence of several men. He drove the demons out of the two men so completely that the townspeople wanted Him to never come back. His disciples and others were right there when the woman's illness was cured, and five people, besides Jesus, were in the room when the little girl was brought back to life.

In this lesson, Matthew records a miracle where Jesus healed two blind men simply by touching them. He was able to do that because of the miraculous power given to Him by God. Others may believe what they want, but believers are confident that their Redeemer can perform miracles. Praise God from whom all blessings—and miracles—flow!

STUDY GUIDE

All the miracles had a purpose—to prove that God is like no one else, to show that He has complete control of creation because He is its source, and to convince us that if He can do all these miraculous things, nothing in our lives is too hard for Him to handle.[44]

How about you? Do you believe the miracles are what the Bible says they were? Are there miracles today? Why does man no longer have the ability to heal in the same way that Jesus did? Jesus said in John 14:12 that those who followed Him would be able to do more than He did.

Opening Questions

1. Blindness was a serious problem in the Near East in the time of Jesus, and it continues to be so today. Why was that the case then, and why does it continue today?

2. There seems to be a discrepancy between the passages recorded in Mark and Luke. Mark 10:46 states, "Then they reached

[44] "Are the Miracles To Be Taken Literally?," https://www.gotquestions.org/miracles-literal.html.

Jericho, and as Jesus and his disciples left town" while Luke 18:35 says, "As Jesus drew near to Jericho." The Gospel writers say either they reached a town, or they left a town. See if you can explain this seeming discrepancy.

3. What is another variation in the Gospel of Matthew versus the Gospels of Mark and Luke?

Questions Leading Up to the Performance of the Miracle

4. What do you know about or what can you find out about the city of Jericho?

5. What did the blind men know immediately about Jesus?

6. Read Ezekiel 34:23–24 along with Matthew 9:27. What were the two blind men really saying about Jesus when they called Him Son of David? You may find both a concrete meaning and an unspoken meaning as you consider that name.

7. Using either your own understanding or any resource available to you, consider the word *mercy.*

    a. Give a definition of *mercy.*
    b. How has God shown His mercy to you?
    c. Some organized religions believe that all people will go to heaven since God is a loving God. However, John 14:6 indicates something different. After reading the verse from John, explain how God is being merciful when He chooses to cast some into everlasting punishment and

reward others with eternal life. Is He being merciful or just or both in these actions?

Questions about the Miracle

Matthew 9:27–31 (also Mark 10:46–52, Luke 18:35–43) Note: Matthew is the only Gospel that refers to *two* blind men.

8. Read Mark 10:46–48 and answer the following:

    a. Provide a list of all the people in these verses.
    b. What was the first response of the blind men?
    c. What was the response from the crowd, and what did that say about them?
    d. What was the second response of the blind men, and what did that say about them?

9. Read Exodus 33:19 and Romans 9:15. Explain what God meant and Paul repeated in the verse from Exodus that Paul quoted in Romans.

10. What do you think the two men sought when they asked for mercy? That is, go beyond the statement itself and tell why they thought they might receive mercy.

11. Jesus did not respond directly about addressing their need. Rather He said, "Do you believe I can make you see?" What purpose or purposes did Jesus have for asking that question?

Summary Questions

12. Since John referred to all the miracles as signs, what do you think blindness was from the standpoint of a sign? Why did you answer the way you did?

13. How would being born again relate to the miracle in this lesson?

14. Read 2 Peter 1:5–9.

    a. Make a list of the attributes of a Christian that Peter expected of believers.
    b. How do these verses speak to the topic of the miracle for this lesson?

15. How did this miracle affect the following:

    a. the one who performed the miracle
    b. the ones on whom the miracle was performed
    c. those who witnessed the miracle

16. Read the quote below and answer the following.

    a. Who is the god referred to in this quote?
    b. Find a reference in the New Testament that uses a different word or words for the god referred to in the quote below.

"To open their eyes and turn them from darkness to light" (Acts 26:18). Would that multitudes all around, blinded by the god of this world, might come to experience the healing of Christ's touch?[45]

[45] Lockyer, "The Miracle of Two Blind Men," 185.

LESSON 17
Jesus Heals a Mute Man and a Paralytic

Jesus healed the deaf, the blind, the mute, the ill, the paralyzed, the demon-possessed, and even raised the dead. Jesus performed thirty-seven miracles according to the Gospels. As phenomenal as that might be, think about this: Jesus was on earth, doing His ministry, for about three years. If you put an annual average to His miracles, it means that Jesus performed approximately twelve miracles each year. With that average in mind, the number of miracles used for this study is most likely only a minute number of the miracles that He actually performed. It also tells that God had the Gospel writers pen only those miracles that He wanted to be recorded.

Thinking about those numbers brings to mind the miracles themselves: which of the difficulties affected a person's lifestyle the most? That is, which might be considered most damaging to a person? Or put another way, which disease would an average person most want healed? Would it be (1) being deaf, (2) being blind, (3) being mute, (4) having a life-threatening or limiting disease, (5) being paralyzed, or (6) being demon-possessed? Being *demon-possessed* would be most debilitating since that would mean that Satan had won and would keep a person in his grasp from here to eternity.

While pondering that, some people came to mind who were

under one or more of the conditions listed. One might argue that Charles Colson was controlled by evil when he served in Richard Nixon's White House, but he built a prison ministry that is even stronger today than it was when he was alive. Regarding being ill with a life-threatening illness, James Boice, a minister of Tenth Presbyterian Church in Philadelphia, loved the Lord until the day he died of incurable cancer. Joni Eareckson Tada is a remarkable artist and apologist for the Lord even though she has been a quadriplegic since her teenage years. The apostle Paul had a "thorn in his side," something we do not know the meaning of, but it was something that the Lord never took from Him. Samson, the last judge of Israel, was blinded and yet he drew strength from God to serve Him with one final act dedicated to the Lord.

These were/are all men and women of God, but they all had something that might have held back the average person. What separates one person from another when someone can overcome a handicap or tragedy like those listed above while another gives up and stops trying? From the believer's standpoint, it must be the power he or she derives from God, Jesus Christ, and the Holy Spirit. There simply is no other answer! There are no unknowns as to why one flourishes and another does not, and there is no chance to overcome issues both here on earth and in heaven without Jesus being alive in one's heart.

What about you? What would happen if you lost your sight, your hearing, your ability to speak, or your ability to get up and walk? Would you feel sorry for yourself and decide that all was lost? Or would you call on the power that can overcome obstacles in any life when a person says yes to our Savior and Lord Jesus Christ?

We all should pray that we would be among the faithful who would turn any physical or mental problem over to the Great

Physician and would do everything in our power to serve Him the way He desires to be served.

STUDY GUIDE

Opening Question for Both Miracles

1. *Challenge.* See if you can find a verse or verses in the Bible that demonstrate that demonic workings and sicknesses were different. Provide book, chapter, and verse(s).

Questions Leading Up to the First Miracle (Jesus Heals a Mute Man)

2. At the same time, do demons have the ability to cause physical afflictions? Explain your answer whether it is yes or no. If it is yes, provide a Bible verse or verses that demonstrate that truth.

3. This may seem to be a very straightforward question, but why would it have been such a challenge for a person to be mute in the time of Jesus?

4. Scan the following scriptures and tell what they all have in common: John 9:1–14, Mark 1:21–27, Mark 1:29–31, Mark 3:1–6, Luke 13:10–17, Luke 14:1–6, and John 5:1–15. Why is that important?

Questions about the First Miracle (Jesus Heals a Mute Man)

Matthew 9:32–34

5. The ESV says that the man in these verses was *demon-oppressed* while some other versions say he was *demon-obsessed.* Would the meaning of the miracle be different based on the two different words? How might the meaning be different?

6. Why did the Pharisees not agree with what the people believed as stated in verse 33?

7. Who is the prince of demons, and what are some other names he goes by?

8. Why did the Pharisees say that Jesus "casts out demons by the prince of demons" (verse 34)?

Questions Leading Up to the Second Miracle (Jesus Heals a Paralyzed Man)

9. What can you find out about the feast that is mentioned here, and is it relevant as to why Jesus had gone to Jerusalem? (The feast is mentioned in John 5:1.)

10. What can you find out about the following:

    a. the Sheep Gate and the overall significance of gates in Jerusalem
    b. Bethesda

11. Historically speaking, Jesus did not perform a lot of miracles in Jerusalem. Why would that have been?

Questions about the Second Miracle (Jesus Heals a Paralyzed Man)

John 5:1–17

12. This miracle was performed on the Sabbath and in a very public place. What reasons might Jesus have had for the timing and the location?

13. Verse 3 states, "In these (colonnades) lay a multitude of invalids—blind, lame, and paralyzed." Rather than healing them all, Jesus chose to heal only this one man (as far as we know). Why would he have limited Himself to one healing and of this person in particular?

14. Compare the verbiage for John 5:3–5 in the KJV to those same verses in other versions of the Bible. What extra information is included in the KJV that is not included in other versions?

15. What makes the KJV seem more accurate as you unfold the reason for this miracle?

16. Jesus asked the man, "Do you want to be healed?" Why do you think He asked that of a man who had been unable to walk for thirty-eight years?

17. After reading verse 7, answer the following:

    a. What does this verse tell you about the man?
    b. What does this verse tell you about the other invalids in the colonnades?
    c. What does this verse instruct believers to do regarding others?

18. Jesus told the man to pick up his bed and walk. There were possibly multiple reasons for Jesus to give that command to the paralyzed man. What might have been one or more of those reasons?

19. Why do you think the man did not know who had healed him?

20. Based on the verses how does one know that this man's malady was caused by a sin of some sort?

21. Read verse 16. Do you agree that what is said there is factual? Why or why not?

22. What does verse 17 mean to you? (You may want to use *The Message* translation.)

Summary Questions

23. *Challenge.* Using your biblical knowledge (or whatever other source you want to use) explain why the Jewish leadership should not have been surprised by what Jesus did in the performance of this and other healing miracles. Provide verses from the Old Testament that prove the point you made.

24. While there are always many attributes one can find in the persons of God and Jesus, what attributes are most obvious in the second miracle? There are at least three that are prominent, maybe more.

25. Doing miracles on the Sabbath was one of the biggest sticking points between Jesus and the Jewish leadership. In your opinion, why did Jesus have the right to change something that had been done for centuries?

26. What does this statement from *All the Miracles of Jesus* by Lockyer mean to you? "The Sanhedrists, the spiritual heads of the nation, had no joy in their cold hearts over the impotent man's relief. All they troubled themselves about was Christ's act of healing on the Sabbath. They forgot that *God has no Sabbath where sin and misery are found*"[46] (emphasis added).

27. How did the miracles affect the following:

    a. the one who performed the miracle
    b. the one for whom the miracle was performed
    c. the people who witnessed the miracle
    d. the people who questioned the miracle

British writer George MacDonald pointed out that John 5:17 gives us a profound insight into our Lord's miracles. Jesus did instantly what the Father is always doing slowly. For example, in nature, as mentioned earlier, the Father is slowly turning water into wine; but

[46] Lockyer, "The Miracle of the Impotent Man," 165–166.

Jesus did it instantly. Through the powers in nature, the Father is healing broken bodies; but Jesus healed them immediately. Nature is repeatedly multiplying bread, from sowing to harvest; but Jesus multiplied it instantly in His own hands.[47]

[47] Wiersbe, "John," https://www.logos.com.

LESSON 18
Jesus Feeds Five Thousand People

When studying the parables of Jesus, one of them may touch one person while a different one may touch another. But for the most part, two or three parables stand out in the minds of Bible readers more than any others do. Those might include the parable of the prodigal son, the parable of the Good Samaritan, and perhaps the parable of the soils. Why are the first two so vivid in the minds of Christians and in fact, in the minds of even the secular world? The answer is they both have universal applications for the believer and the nonbeliever.

Just because they have applications for both groups of people, however, does not mean that those applications are what Jesus intended when he taught them. For the secular reader, the prodigal son parable simply means that someone messed up his life, and someone who was kind welcomed him back into the fold. With the Good Samaritan parable, the understanding of the nonbelieving world is even more universal and has become a byword for how one person should treat another. In fact, this parable is so widespread in its application that there are even Good Samaritan laws that protect a person who may do harm to someone in a situation where they were trying to help.

So why mention parables right in the midst of a study of the miracles of Jesus? Primarily because some of the miracles, like some parables, fall into the category of being well-known and somewhat known by the secular community as well as Christians. While there are many of these types of miracles, two of them, just as with the parables, stand out.

The miracle of turning water into wine is one that is so well-known and popular in the secular world that there are wine stores called Water 2 Wine. Whether the owners of these stores are Christian or not, it would appear that they are missing the mark regarding what the Lord accomplished in performing this miracle. Certainly, He turned water into wine, but most importantly, He proved His sovereignty over nature by turning water into the finest of wines.

The miracle of feeding the 5,000 in this lesson is probably the most well-known miracle and is familiar to many people—both inside and outside the faith. The most prominent explanation for this miracle by those outside the faith is that this is really a story of people sharing with one another. That is, once someone saw that a boy with a few loaves and fishes was sharing with others, all the other people began to do the same. Of course, this takes the miracle out of the realm of that which is impossible to understand into the simplistic arena of people making things happen. While it is good to share with others, those who believe know the truth is that Jesus prayed to God, and the five loaves and two fish turned supernaturally into so much that there were twelve baskets full of bread left over! So even if everyone had shared, would there have been that much extra to be collected?

The miracles of Jesus are just exactly that, miracles. Jesus used them to show who He was and what He was able to do with people and for people who had faith in His power. Those who downplay what the Lord can do are truly traveling down a slippery slope leading nowhere! He can and will do whatever is required to make sure that His will is eventually carried out to the full.

STUDY GUIDE

To feed 5,000 people with five loaves and two fish is indeed miraculous, but the Greek term used in Matthew 14:21 specifies males, and Matthew further emphasizes the point by adding, "Besides women and children." Many Bible scholars believe the actual number fed that day could have been 15,000–20,000 people.[48]

Opening Questions

1. How does this sentence from Vance Havner (a Southern Baptist minister who is known as one of America's most traveled evangelists) address Jesus and the disciples at this point in the ministry, "If you don't come apart and rest, you will come apart."

2. Does that sentence apply to Jesus and the disciples equally or in different ways?

3. How does that sentence apply to believers today—or does it? Please explain.

---

[48] "What can we learn from Jesus' feeding of the 5000?," https://www.gotquestions.org/feeding-the-5000.html.

Questions Leading Up to the Miracle

4. According to Mark 6:14–29, what event had taken place shortly before the feeding of the 5,000?

5. In what ways might the event in Number 4 have changed the focus of Jesus and His ministry?

6. Read Mark 6:7–13 to find out what the apostles were talking to Jesus about in Mark 6:30. You may also want to look at Luke 9:6.

7. What can you determine about the ministry of Jesus when you read Mark 6:31?

8. Because the crowd knew where Jesus was going, they interfered with the time to rest that Jesus and the twelve disciples needed. Why do you think the people were so excited to see Jesus?

Questions about the Miracle

Mark 6:30–44 (also Matthew 14:13–21, Luke 9:10–17, John 6:1–15)

9. Because the rest they needed was interrupted, there are several things one can ask:

    a. What was Jesus's reaction to the people who had gathered to see Him?
    b. What does this tell you about Jesus?
    c. What do you think the disciples might have learned from Jesus's reaction to the interruption?

d. Why do you think Jesus saw the people as sheep without a shepherd? This may have both an obvious and a less obvious answer.
e. What example does it set for believers today?

10. You will need to scan each of the Gospel accounts to answer this question. What does each account say that Jesus did ministry-wise before the actual miracle of feeding the 5,000 occurred?

11. What might be considered positive and negative points regarding the apostles' desire to send the people away so they could get food?

12. Using the John 6:1–15 account of this miracle, answer all parts of questions 12, 13, and 14.

    a. Why did Jesus say what He did to Philip? What does this tell you about Jesus?
    b. What did Philip immediately say to Jesus? What does this tell you about Philip (and the rest of the disciples as well)?
    c. Philip used the term "two hundred denarii" in the ESV while other translations use silver coins or silver pieces. Regardless of the term your version uses, how much money in practical terms was Philip talking about?

13. What did Andrew say to Jesus? What does this tell you about Andrew?

14. John's account of this miracle calls the bread barley loaves. See if you can find out why putting in that detail makes the miracle even more relevant to many of the people who were there that day.

15. Returning to Mark 6:30–44 account of the miracle, why do you think Jesus had the people sit down on green grass and "in groups, by hundreds and by fifties"?

16. Christians believe that Jesus was God incarnate when He was on earth, yet "he [Jesus] looked up to heaven and said a blessing and broke the loaves" (verse 41).

    a. As God incarnate, why would He have done this?
    b. What lesson was being taught to the disciples and to the crowd?
    c. What lesson do His followers today learn from what Jesus did?

17. The loaves and fishes were then distributed, "and they all ate and were satisfied." Considering that was the crux of this miracle, answer the following question. The disciples collected twelve baskets full of bread and fish. What significance could be attached to the number 12 in the Bible?

Summary Questions

18. Make a list of some of the lessons that can and/or should be taken away from the miracle of feeding the 5,000.

19. Which of the lessons are most meaningful to you? Why?

20. How did this miracle affect the following people?

    a. Jesus
    b. the crowd

c. the disciples

d. believers today

21. Read the quote below. Choose one of the referenced scriptures and explain why it is important to you and your life as a believer.

Christians must bring their lives to God in a spirit of obedience and sacrifice, no matter how insignificant they may think their gifts or talents are (Romans 12:1). When doing so, expect God to do far beyond what can be imagined (Ephesians 3:20). Also, Christians should trust that God not only wants to meet the needs of His children, but He wants to lavish His children with spiritual blessings, even to overflowing (Psalm 23:5).[49]

[49] "What can we learn from Jesus' feeding of the 5000?," https://www.gotquestions.org/feeding-the-5000.html.

LESSON 19
Jesus Walks on Water

It has been said that the Bible, while inerrant in the original language, is not exhaustive. What does that mean? It means that every word of the scriptures can be relied on when read and used as God intended, but it also means that God gave the human writers only that which He wanted to give. Consequently, there is much that happened in both the Old Testament and New Testament that is not recorded because God is not ready for us to know all things (1 Corinthians 2:9). Consider the following which are just a few of the mysteries of the Bible. Believers know the what but have no concept of the how.

- *The mystery of the incarnation.* "It is no mystery that God should reveal Himself by speaking from the Heavens, as on Mt. Sinai, but that He should take on the 'Human form' and 'tabernacle' among us that was a great mystery. This He did in the person of Christ (John 1:1–14). So Jesus could say, 'He that hath seen me hath seen the Father'" (John 14:9).[50]

[50] "The Mystery of the Incarnation," *Mysteries of the Bible Pt. 1,* accessed March 1, 2019, www.faithweb.com.

- *The mystery of the divine indwelling.* "This is a great mystery because it is the mystery of the 'New Birth.' The New Birth is wonderful, and it is a wonderful fact. It is the union of the Divine Nature and ours. So that just as Jesus became one with us by His taking on human nature, so we become one with Him by taking on the Divine Nature. ... We are just as much a part of Christ as the members of the body are a part of the body" (1 Corinthians 12:12).[51]
- *The mystery of the translation of the living saints.* "This is the greatest of all mysteries because it reveals something that reason never dreamed of. According to reason the common lot of man is to die, but to be taken off this earth and translated to heaven without dying was never thought of until revealed to Paul."[52]

These, of course, are all theological mysteries that have been studied, restudied, and debated throughout the centuries. These mysteries make one's head swim because of the depth of each of them, and readers may or may not become involved in a deep discussion of any of them during their lifetime. At the same time, there are other mysteries that are thought of often, and many of those are the ones studied in *The Miracles of Jesus.* To that end, consider these two miracles.

Jesus feeding the 5,000 (and the 4,000). What is the first reaction to this if Jesus is thought of from a purely human, logical standpoint? There is no way it could have ever happened! It is so

[51] "The Mystery of the Divine Indwelling," Mysteries of The Bible Pt. 1, www.faithweb.com.

[52] Clarence Larkin, "The Mystery of the Translation of the Living Saints," www.blueletterbible.org/study/larkin/dt/27.cfm.

much easier to believe what skeptics have believed and still believe: the people saw one young boy offer to share what little food he had, so all the others felt guilty because of what the young boy did and did the same. Certainly, that is a remarkable story of compassion and sharing with your fellow man, but where is the mystery in that? In some way, supernaturally, and mysteriously, Jesus turned very little into a whole lot!

Jesus walking on water. One might appear to be walking on water if the water is very shallow and the feet seem to be on top, or they might appear to be walking on water because of stones that lie just below the surface. But no one could possibly walk on top of the water of a huge lake, particularly a lake that is tempest tossed because that is simply impossible. But Jesus did! Jesus, God incarnate, is not only the creator of all, but He is also continuing as the master of all, even nature. The believer doesn't have to grasp the mysteries of the Lord but simply accept them! He can do all because He is all. Praise be to the God who is the creator and ruler of all things—the straightforward and the mysterious.

STUDY GUIDE

In Oscar Hammerstein and Richard Rodgers's musical *Carousel*, the song "You'll Never Walk Alone" encourages the main character with the words, "When you walk through a storm, hold your head up high, and don't be afraid of the dark. At the end of a storm, there's a golden sky and the sweet silver song of a lark. Walk on through the wind, walk on through the rain though your dreams be tossed and blown. Walk on, walk on with hope in your heart, and you'll never walk alone."

Opening Questions

1. Is there anything you call on in times of stress to deal with what's going on in your life? This can be a song, a hymn, a poem, a Bible verse, a secular or religious saying, and so forth.

2. "He performed no miracles for His own relief when suffering intense anguish in Gethsemane, when being beaten by Roman soldiers, or when hanging on the stake."[53] What does that statement mean to you?

3. Referring back to the miracle of the feeding of the 5,000, what was the reason(s) for Jesus performing that miracle?

4. The disciples had just completed a mission trip and reported back to Jesus regarding their success. Next, they were part of the feeding of the 5,000. Surely, they would have been on a spiritual high. What can be the dangers associated with a spiritual high?

Questions Leading Up to the Miracle

Mark 6:45–46

5. Jesus and the disciples had just experienced one of the greatest miracles, yet according to the *ESV*, Jesus "made the disciples get into the boat and go before him to the other side." This would have been a time of celebration for them all.

---

[53] Martin G. Collins, "The Miracles of Jesus Part One, 3. What was the main purpose of Christ's miracles?," accessed March 1, 2019, https://www.cgg.org/index.cfm/library/biblestudy/id/1173/miracles-jesus-christ.htm.

a. What one or more reasons do you think Jesus had for insisting that his disciples go on without Him?
b. Both Matthew and Mark used the word *made* when they told this part of the story. Why would a loving Savior have used such a harsh word with those to whom He was closest?

6. Again, Jesus had just completed this fantastic miracle, but He went off on His own to pray. What were the motivating factors about that move of Jesus?

7. How were Jesus's deity and His humanity combined as He went by Himself to pray?

Questions about the Miracle

Mark 6:45–52 (also Matthew 14:22–33, John 6:16–21)

8. At the end of the time Jesus spent in prayer, where were the disciples and in what condition?

9. Since Jesus is God incarnate and since God is omniscient, Jesus would have known what was going to take place. Why then did He intentionally send them out in a boat on rough seas?

10. What did the fourth watch of the night equate to in clock time, and approximately how much time would have elapsed between the disciples beginning their trip across the sea and Jesus appearing to them?

11. Considering your answer to question 10 above, what must the mental state of the disciples have been like?

12. One of the more interesting statements in this miracle is when Mark wrote, “He meant to pass them by.” After all the disciples had been through since they left Jesus on the shore, why would Jesus have intentionally ignored them?

13. In your opinion what response was Jesus hoping for or expecting from the disciples when they were in peril?

14. Mark 6:51 states, “And they were utterly astounded.”

    a. What was the main thing or things that astounded them?
    b. What is a reason or reasons why they should not have been astounded?
    c. What is it about Jesus and the Word of God that continues to astound you today?

15. This miracle demonstrates several miracles within the miracle for which it is named. List the miracles and tell which of them is the most miraculous to you and why.

16. Did the disciples fail this latest test given to them by Jesus? Why or why not?

Summary Questions

17. *Challenge.* Herbert Lockyer in his book *All the Miracles of the Bible* believes that there are three unique points made about

Jesus in this miracle. Two of those have to do with Jesus as an individual, and one of them has to do with the disciples.[54] They can all be found in Matthew 14:23–33. See if you can mirror what Lockyer thinks or find points of your own.

18. *Challenge.* Think about this miracle. Attempt to write a real-life scenario that might line up with what happened in the miracle of Jesus walking on the water. Include what might be representative of the sea, the storm on the sea, Peter getting out of the boat, Peter beginning to sink, and Peter's rescue by Jesus. This will require creative thinking.

19. *Challenge.* Skim Mark 4:35–41 along with Mark 6:45–52.

    a. What similarities do you see in the two sets of scripture?
    b. What was Jesus trying to teach the disciples based on what is told in the two scriptures?

20. How did this miracle affect the following people:

    a. the one who performed the miracle
    b. the one for whom the miracle was performed
    c. the ones who witnessed the miracle

21. Part of Psalm 46 is quoted below; it is indicative of what so many of the psalms are about. Reflect on the Psalms overall and share one that is particularly comforting to you. Why is it comforting, and when do you find yourself turning to it?

---

[54] Lockyer, "The Miracle of Walking on the Water," 200–203.

God's Word Speaks

"God is our refuge and strength, a very present help in trouble. Therefore we will not fear though the earth gives way, though the mountains be moved into the heart of the sea, though its waters roar and foam, though the mountains tremble at its swelling" (Psalm 46:1–3, ESV).

LESSON 20

Jesus Heals Woman's Demon-Possessed Daughter

The nineteen miracles performed by Jesus so far in this study create quite a resume, and His disciples were right there with Him witnessing everything Jesus did. Therefore, having been part of all that, it should make sense that they were understanding more and more of what Jesus was all about. After all, two miracles were beyond belief for any ordinary man or woman: Jesus had fed 5,000 men with five loaves and two fish, and Jesus had walked on the waters of the Sea of Galilee in a raging storm. However, as shown by their rescue on the sea the disciples really were not much closer to "getting it" than they had been.

In another miracle on the sea, Jesus and the disciples, after a long day, got in a boat, set sail on the Sea of Galilee, and headed for the other side of the lake. The human side of Jesus was exhausted, so He went to the back of the boat, laid down, and immediately went to sleep. Shortly thereafter a storm arose, so severe that the disciples feared their end was near. But they cried out to Jesus, having no idea what He might be able to do to help, and then miraculously, He calmed the sea with the words, "Peace! Be still!" Jesus's statement to them after the sea had become perfectly calm was "Why are you so afraid? Have you still no faith?" The disciples had now experienced two supernatural events on the sea, yet they were still not capable of grasping the omnipotence of the Savior.

There was much more to what the disciples had observed than just the miracles. They had seen how Jesus related to people at all levels. They had seen how those people were drawn to Him and were willing to follow Him just to get a glimpse of Him or hear Him or touch His garment. They had experienced Jesus in the presence of people who they had previously thought were unclean or beneath them. And they had witnessed Jesus taking on the very power structure of the Jewish nation. Why then did they not get what was going on? That needs to be answered through self-examination.

Are people, even believers, any different or any better today? Are sincere Christians any more apt to understand the power of Jesus than the disciples? While it is a convenient truth to say Christians in the twenty-first century have not had the personal relationship with Jesus that the disciples had, it is a much less convenient truth to admit that today's followers of Christ have more than the disciples did. How can that be? First, the same Hebrew scriptures they had are in any Bible today. Second, the New Testament scriptures are available now but were not available then. Third, Jesus is still walking with those who follow Him even though it is through the power of the Holy Spirit. Fourth, there are over 2,000 years of church history proving how powerful the Word of God is, and finally, all sorts of Christian fellowship provide growth in the truth of His Word. So rather than less than the disciples had, today's Christians have more!

Before God's chosen of today get too full of themselves, they need to understand that people still do not have a full grasp of the truth of God's Word or of who Jesus really is. Many individuals have too many preconceived notions of the way they want things to be, and many individuals are less involved in the deep study of God's Word than they need to be if a sincere search for truth is what they want.

Just as will be seen in the next miracle, Christ will be there for those who need Him. He will give comfort, peace, joy, and healing. And even though He is no longer here on earth, Jesus left His spirit for those who believe. We can have everything the disciples had and more!

STUDY GUIDE

Opening Questions

1. The verses from Matthew 14:34–36 start with "And when they had crossed over." From where did they cross over?

2. They were going to Gennesaret from where they had been. See what you can find out about this town: location, significance, commerce, and any other details.

3. *Challenge.* Just as the woman with the bleeding disorder, many were healed when they touched the fringe on Jesus's garment. While that may sound a bit mystical or magical, there was a sound theological background as to why they did what they did. See what you can find out about a *tzitzit* and why that part of Jewish clothing was so important.

Questions Leading Up to the Miracle

4. Prior to the next miracle, Jesus engaged in teaching moments both with the Jewish leaders and the people. Starting in the first verses of Matthew 15, Jesus used what might at first seem to be a convoluted example to meet the challenge of the Pharisees and scribes. However, Jesus was at His best.

    a. For what did the Pharisees and scribes condemn Jesus and His disciples?
    b. How did Jesus counter the Pharisees and scribes in verse 3, and why would Jesus's statement have been so offensive to them?
    c. What was Jesus saying to the Jewish leaders in verses 4–6? Look up the word *corban* to help with your answer.

5. Read Acts 10:9–16. Do you see similarities between those verses and Matthew 15:11? Explain.

6. Jesus said in Matthew 15:14, "They are blind guides." To whom was He referring, and why would He have called them blind guides?

7. Where and why were the Pharisees and scribes missing the point?

Questions about the Miracle

Matthew 15:21–29 (also Mark 7:24–30)

8. Matthew 15:21 says, "Jesus went away from there and withdrew to the district of Tyre and Sidon."

a. Where was *there* and why did Jesus go away from that place?
b. What was the significance of His going into the district of Tyre and Sidon? (You will need to locate these cities on a map to help with your answer.)

9. The woman in this miracle is referred to as a Syro-Phoenician or Canaanite. See what you can find that would support her being called either of those names.

10. Why would it be unusual that the woman called Jesus both Lord and Son of David?

11. The woman came to Jesus with a sincerely spoken request, "But He did not answer her a word" (verse 23). Why do you think He did not respond to her at first?

12. Look at the disciples' response in verse 23. Why did they respond the way they did? How you answer will depend on which version of the Bible you use (especially if you use the wording from *The Message*).

13. What is the woman's next response, and what does that tell you about her?

14. This lesson's miracle gets still more interesting in verses 26 and 27, and there are several questions that need to be answered regarding those verses.

    a. Who is Jesus referring to when He speaks of the *children*?
    b. What is Jesus speaking of when He speaks of the *children's bread*?

c. Who is Jesus speaking of when He speaks of the *dogs*?
d. What does the woman mean by what she said in verse 27?

15. What did the woman not ask for in these verses?

16. Answer the following questions referring to verse 28:

a. Why did Jesus see the woman's faith as being so great?
b. Does the level of her faith remind you of another miracle studied that involved a woman? Who was that woman? What was the outcome?
c. By implication, to whose faith do you think Jesus was comparing the woman's faith?

Summary Questions

17. What two great rewards did the woman receive?

18. What does the woman's attitude teach us?

19. Summarize the following statement in your own words. "Her unparalleled faith in Christ proved that it is not blood, proving the true Abraham lineage, but faith, and, tried by that test, she was a spiritual daughter of Abraham. If she is a Gentile in nationality, she is an Israelite in disposition."[55]

20. *Challenge.* Find an Old Testament verse or verses that verify what is stated in question 19.

---

[55] Lockyer, "The Miracle of the Syro-Phoenician Woman's Daughter," 206.

21. How did this miracle affect the following:

    a. the one who performed the miracle
    b. the one on whom the miracle was performed
    c. the ones who witnessed the miracle
    d. the one who requested the miracle

22. Read the quote below. Lockyer states this may have been Jesus's "first convert from heathenism." Does this statement conflict with the fact that the woman at the well and her townspeople had come to Christ?

The Syro-Phoenician woman was another of the "other sheep" not of the Jewish fold which Jesus said He would bring. Probably she was His first convert from heathenism.[56]

[56] Lockyer, 207.

LESSON 21
Jesus Heals a Deaf Man

In Genesis 12:3 the Lord said, "I will bless those who bless you, and him who dishonors you I will curse, and in you all the families of the earth shall be blessed." This happened when Abraham was first called to leave his country and go to a land that the Lord would show him, and it demonstrates from the very start of the Jewish nation that somehow every nation and all the peoples of the world would be blessed through the line of Abraham.

Turning to Daniel 7:14, the author of that book recorded this, "And to him was given dominion and glory and a kingdom, that all peoples, nations, and languages should serve him; his dominion is an everlasting dominion, which shall not pass away, and his kingdom one that shall not be destroyed." Once again, there is no room for doubt that God has always intended that He is the God of all mankind and not just of the Jews.

Isaiah 49:6 continues this same truth, "It is too light a thing that you should be my servant to raise up the tribes of Jacob and to bring back the preserved of Israel; I will make you as a light for the nations, that my salvation may reach to the end of the earth." Since Israel was one nation, does this not imply that God would eventually send One who would come to redeem all the people of the earth even those people who may be seen as having no right to the kingdom?

But Hosea 2:23 may put it most beautifully of all when it states, "And I will sow her for myself in the land. And I will have mercy on No Mercy, and I will say to Not My People, 'You are my people;' and he shall say, 'You are my God.'" This means that Gentiles—those who did not originally have God's mercy and who were not His people—are now included with all the rights and privileges of the chosen people.

Notice something familiar in all these verses: the words used—*families*, *nations*, and *people*—are all plural words which means that God through Jesus, through His disciples, through the apostles, and now through believers wants to call all people to Himself! If it had not been for the wonderful grace that has been given by the sacrifice of God's own Son, Gentiles would still be wallowing in sin with no hope of anything beyond this life other than the grave and eternal punishment.

The message from the miracle of healing the Syro-Phoenician woman's daughter is a beautiful remembrance of the promises of God in the Old Testament. She was a person who was a Gentile, and at some level, she knew she was not chosen. However, at a greater level—a salvation level—she knew that she, a Gentile, had the same rights and privileges as the biological children of Israel. She called on Jesus as if she were a Jew, and because of her perseverance and faith, Jesus healed her daughter.

Although the lesson of the Syro-Phoenician woman may have been different in some ways from other miracles, it was the same as the entire story in the Lord's Holy Word: God's chosen people are those that accept Jesus as Savior and Lord, and the chosen people are not called from a particular race or ethnicity. The Samaritan woman at the well, the healing of the centurion's servant, the willingness of Jesus to go into non-Jewish territory, and all the promises from the Old Testament show again and again that all who have faith will sit at the heavenly banquet when their time on earth is done. The story of the Syro-Phoenician woman is one more story in a long string of stories that help all believers know they belong to Jesus Christ.

STUDY GUIDE

How open are you to God's Word being shared with everyone, particularly with those who may disagree on Christian theology or Christian practices? Are the following groups excluded from your thinking when you consider sharing Jesus with others: Muslims, Jehovah's Witnesses, the Church of the Latter-Day Saints, Catholics, agnostics, and atheists? Well, Jesus wasn't uncomfortable or reluctant, and it is the believer's call to do what He did!

Questions Before the Questions

How do you respond to the issue in the quote above? Is there a group or groups with whom you hesitate to share God's Word? What group(s) and why?

Opening Questions

1. Warren Wiersbe in *The Bible Exposition Commentary* refers to the Decapolis as a "Rome away from Rome." Why would he call it that? What might that tell about the area that would have led Jesus to minister there?

2. As a review, list the type of action(s) Jesus took to cause the following miracles to happen. For example, when Jesus raised Jairus's daughter, He took her by the hand and told her to rise from the bed. Give as much information as you would like on each of them.

    a. Turning water into wine
    b. Healing the centurion's servant
    c. Calming the storm on the sea
    d. Healing the woman with a bleeding disorder

Questions Leading Up to the Miracle

3. *Challenge.* The beginning section of scripture for this lesson (Mark 7:31) says, "Then he returned from the region of Tyre and went through Sidon to the Sea of Galilee." This seems strange since Sidon was about twenty miles north of Tyre where Jesus healed the Phoenician woman's daughter. See what you can find out that would tell why Jesus went north to Sidon to get south to the Sea of Galilee.

4. For what reason do you think Jesus went back into the Decapolis area where He sent the demons into the pigs causing the citizenry to want him to leave and not return?

5. Read about the man mentioned in Matthew 9:32 alongside the one spoken of in Mark 7:32. What difference or differences can you see when comparing the verses? What might this tell you about the nature of physical disabilities or problems?

Questions about the Miracle

Mark 7:31–37

6. Read verse 32 again and tell what this miracle has in common with another miracle that has been studied. There may be one or more previous miracles that come to mind.

7. What can be gathered from the fact that the man was completely deaf yet had a speech impediment (some ability to speak)?

8. Continuing with what is said in verse 32 answer the following:

    a. What were the people who brought the man expecting to happen when "they begged him [Jesus] to lay his hand on him?"
    b. In your opinion do you think what they expected and what the woman with the bleeding issue expected were the same or different? Explain.

9. Why did Jesus take the man aside from the crowd to deal with him privately?

10. Jesus touched the man's ear first and then his tongue. From a purely physical standpoint, why does doing what He did in that order make sense?

11. After spitting on His own hand, Jesus touched the man's tongue. Although this may seem unsavory or unsanitary, see if you can find out why Jesus might have done that, especially as it pertains to the culture of His day.

12. Jesus then did three things: (a) He looked up to heaven, (b) He sighed, and (c) He spoke to the man. What was the meaning of each of these actions?

13. Continuing with the word *sighed* in the previous question, the word used here is the same as another word, *groan,* used in Romans 8:23 and 8:26. Explain what the purpose of the word *groan* was in these two passages and how that purpose compares with the usage of *sighed* in Mark 7:34.

14. Mark records that Jesus used the word Ephphatha and then explained what that word meant. Why would he both use the word and define it?

Summary Questions

15. Although this miracle had the effect of physically opening the man's ears so that he could hear, what outcome did Jesus hope would occur in the understanding of the disciples?

16. Thinking about the previous question, provide a verse where Jesus said basically the same thing.

17. What major difference can you see between the outcome of this miracle and the outcome of the previous miracle when Jesus was in the Decapolis? (See the first verses of Mark 5.)

18. How did this miracle affect the following:

    a. the one on whom the miracle was performed
    b. the ones who witnessed the miracle

c. others who witnessed the miracle (use Matthew 15:31)

19. Read the quote at the bottom. Tell which method Jesus used to heal is most impressive to you.

20. Continuing with the quote below, what aspect of Jesus's ministry (think beyond the miracles if you want) has given you cause to marvel the most?

There was nothing stereotyped about His methods. Some were healed in a crowd, others in solitude. Others were healed by a word, or by a touch, or by spittle, or by clay. There were others healed at a distance, and others were present. One method of healing was instantaneous, while another was healed gradually. Because of His wisdom and omnipotence, He works in ways He deems best.[57]

[57] Lockyer, "The Miracle of the Deaf and Dumb Man of Decapolis," 208.

LESSON 22
Jesus Feeds 4,000 People

In 1 Peter 3:15, Peter makes this powerful statement, "But in your hearts honor Christ the Lord as holy, always being prepared to make a defense to anyone who asks you for a reason for the hope that is in you; yet do it with gentleness and respect." What could be more gratifying for a Christian than to be able to defend the truth on the spot to whoever might be challenging the faith believers hold so dear? Most believers can give some answers in some situations, but there are too many times that words fail because they are not written on the heart.

In the study of the miracles of Jesus so far, several questions have been asked that broach the topic of defending the Gospel. One of the things that causes concern is why facts about the same miracle may have been recorded differently by the four Gospel authors. Assumptions that have been made about this topic include the following:

- The authors' perceptions of a situation differed;
- One author omitted something that was important to another author;
- Each Gospel focused on a different aspect of Christ, and

- As the true author of His Word, God directed each Gospel author to write what He put on their individual hearts.

The authors wrote no differently than any author might write, and any person might look at a situation and see something different than another. That is just the way human nature is, but it doesn't make one person's take on a topic any better or truer than another's. It simply makes them different.

The goal, therefore, is to become a true *apologist* for the faith. One of the biggest challenges is to be able to answer questions about the consistency of the Bible because critics of the Bible are always anxious to tell how "this part of the Bible" is not consistent with "that part of the Bible." The miracle in this lesson is one of the miracles both Bible critics and liberal theologians point to when they are attempting to prove that the Bible is not all it claims to be.

Jesus and His disciples were involved in a meal where they fed 5,000 men plus women and children with five loaves and two fish, and then a relatively short time thereafter, they hosted another meal where they fed 4,000 men plus women and children with seven loaves and a few small fish. As a believer in the inerrancy of the scripture, one can easily accept that these were two distinct, different meals that the Lord miraculously caused to happen. However, those who are more skeptical of His Holy Word have decided that these are the same events and are simply recorded in a different way by different authors. It seems those people fail to grasp that God through Jesus could have performed two similar miracles in a very short frame of reference.

In the study of the miracle in this lesson, an attempt will be made to dissect why liberal thinkers believe that Jesus did miraculous feedings on two occasions, not one. This question hopefully will be answered, "What makes one event unique and different from the other?" By the time the lesson has ended, there will be one more arrow in the apologetic quiver that will help Christians become stronger apologists for the Word of God.

STUDY GUIDE

What does it mean that the Bible is infallible? The word *infallible* means "incapable of error." If something is infallible, it is never wrong and thus absolutely trustworthy. Similarly, the word *inerrant,* also applied to Scripture, means "free from error." Simply put, the Bible never fails.[58]

Opening Questions

1. Since the miracle of this lesson sounds like another miracle (feeding of the 4,000 versus feeding of the 5,000), this first question deals with the inerrancy of scripture. What does each of the following verses say about the subject of inerrancy?

    a. 2 Timothy 3:16–17
    b. 2 Peter 1:20–21
    c. Hebrews 6:18

2. The Bible is inerrant in the original language. What does that mean?

3. What does "the Bible is inerrant but nonexhaustive" mean?

[58] "What does it mean that the Bible is infallible?," https://www.gotquestions.org/Bible-infallible.html.

4. Where is the Bible shown as nonexhaustive in the study of the miracles?

Questions Leading Up to the Miracle

5. See what you can find out about the elapsed time between the feeding of the 5,000 and the feeding of the 4,000.

6. In Matthew 15:21–39, the writer recorded the healing of the Canaanite (Syro-Phoenician) woman, the healing of many, and then the feeding of the 4,000. Mark 7:24–8:9 deals with the Syro-Phoenician woman, then the of healing the deaf man, and follows that with the feeding of the 4,000.

    a. What did Matthew write about in the section that deals with the healing of many? Make a list of all the things Matthew mentioned.
    b. Why would Matthew use a general statement about healing many while Mark dealt with the healing of a specific person? Does this show an inconsistency in the scripture? Explain.

7. What do you learn about the following in Matthew 15:32 and Mark 8:2?

    a. Jesus
    b. the crowd who had gathered to hear Him speak
    c. how this speaks to believers today

Questions about the Miracle

Mark 8:1–9 (also Matthew 15:30–38)

8. What do Matthew 15:33 and Mark 8:4 tell you about the disciples?

9. What is so remarkable (not a positive thing) about the disciples in the previous question? (Think about the miracle of feeding the 5,000.)

10. Thinking about yourself, in what situation or situations are you most likely to mirror what the disciples were like?

11. How many loaves of bread and fish did the disciples have that were used to feed the crowd?

12. Mark 8:8 states that the people were satisfied. What does that mean physically and spiritually?

13. *Challenge*. The premise behind this lesson is that the feeding of the 5,000 and the feeding of the 4,000 are two distinct events in the Bible. Various sources point out as many as 10 to 12 differences between the two events, and perhaps there are more. How many can you identify? (Really dig into this one and see what differences there are. This is a great exercise for would-be apologists!)

Summary Questions

Lockyer quotes C. J. Ellicott in Ellicott's *Commentary on the Whole Bible*, "It is significant that there, as so often before, the display of miraculous power in its highest form originates not in answer to a challenge, or as being offered as a proof of a Divine mission, but simply from compassion."[59]

14. Look at the quote above. Think beyond the miracles and provide one or more times with scripture's support where Jesus's words or actions came strictly from compassion.

15. Read Matthew 16:9–10 and Mark 8:18–21. What do these two scriptures prove absolutely?

16. In both the feeding of the 5,000 and now in the feeding of the 4,000, there were twelve baskets and seven baskets of leftover bread, respectively.

    a. First, what is the meaning of the bread in both stories? Think of this from both a physical and a spiritual context.
    b. Second, what is the meaning of the leftovers in both stories? Again, think physically and spiritually.

17. How does this miracle validate what Jesus said in John 6:35?

18. How did the miracle affect the following:

    a. the one who performed the miracle
    b. the ones for whom the miracle was performed
    c. the ones (disciples) who witnessed the miracle

---

[59] Lockyer, "The Miracle of Feeding the 4000," 210.

19. How often do you think about what the Lord has done for you? (Reference the quote below.)

Sometimes we find ourselves doubting the Lord's concern for us and His ability to meet our needs. If we were to remember what He has done for us, particularly in rescuing us from sin when we were hopelessly lost, we would find ourselves more apt to trust that He will provide. Think on what the Lord has done for you, and trust that He will come through again because He loves you.[60]

[60] "Feeding 4000," www.ligonier.org.

LESSON 23

Jesus Heals a Blind Man at the Pool of Bethsaida

Jesus Heals a Man Blind Since Birth

If you have ever visited one of the great caverns of America, you most likely came to a room somewhere deep in the cavern's bowels, and the guide warned you that all the lights were going to be turned off. Why were all the lights going to be extinguished? Because the guide wanted you to experience total darkness. When that happened, you found out that the guide had not exaggerated—it was so dark you could not see your hand in front of your face, and your eyes did not adjust to the darkness as they might in a darkened room. If you have had that experience, how did you feel?

Some of you may have been amazed that anything or anywhere could be that dark. Some may have been a bit scared and worried the guide might not be able to find the switch or that the power would have been lost permanently. Others may have wanted the lights turned back on so they could get on with the rest of the tour. But did any of you think about blind people and the fact that total darkness is their world? The lights never go on for them, and their eyes never get accustomed to the light.

However, is that total darkness which blind people experience any different for one who loses their sight at some point in life versus someone who never knows sight? The former would know what they were missing while the latter really would not. Even if you told someone born blind what a tree looked like, that person would have no reference point to know what you were talking about. But the person who was born with normal sight and then lost it would know what they were missing by no longer being able to see a tree. Which is worse?

The study of the miracles in this lesson is about one blind person who had his sight when born while the other talks about one born blind. For both men, blindness in and of itself would be tragedy enough. As shown before though, the miracles Jesus performed were about much more than just healing a physical illness or malady. The Gospel writers, and particularly John, were intent on letting the readers know that the problem a person faced was a sign of something much greater. There was always a spiritual element to each of the physical manifestations.

One who is blind cannot literally see the physical world, but one who is blind spirituality cannot see the truth of God's Word. This is what Jesus preached so strongly to many of the Jewish leaders of His day. They had all the head knowledge they could possibly have about the scriptures, but they did not understand that head knowledge was not the primary thing God wanted the people to have.

Think about the blindness of some people in the Bible. Cain brought what he thought God wanted, yet he missed the mark. Saul was anointed king over Israel but lost his way when his desires took precedence over God's will. The priests in the latter-day Old Testament knew all the rules, but they forgot about teaching the truth to the people. The religious leaders in the New Testament had

613 laws to govern their daily lives, but they forgot about the heart meaning of the Ten Commandments.

Those people may have all been able to see physically, but all of them were blind spiritually, and things have not changed over time. All believers, at one time or another, may have lost their way and depended on what they desired rather than on God's will. The challenge is to overcome the blindness of the world with the vision of Christ. When followers do that, they will be doing what Micah 6:8 says God wants us to do. "He has told you, O man, what is good; and what does the Lord require of you but to do justice, and to love kindness, and to walk humbly with your God?"

STUDY GUIDE

But Jesus was not a miraculous therapeutic machine: He dealt with individuals individually and personally and not in a mechanical way.[61]

Opening Questions for Both Miracles

1. Review the quote above and answer the following:
    a. In the study of the miracles reviewed so far, provide your favorite example of Jesus interacting with an individual and explain why it is your favorite.
    b. In the study of the miracles reviewed so far, provide an example of how Jesus did not treat people in a mechanical way.

[61] Lockyer, "The Miracle of the Bethsaida Blind Man," 211.

2. Herbert Lockyer in his book *All the Miracles of the Bible* says, "It is the general law under the government of God that suffering is the result of sin."

    a. Do you agree with that statement? Explain whether you agree or disagree.
    b. What does the statement *not* say about illness?

Questions Leading Up to Both Miracles

3. As another way of review, why would Jesus have been particularly interested in healing blind people from a spiritual lesson standpoint?

4. What group would He have been addressing with these miracles (healing the blind), and why would He have been addressing that group in particular?

Questions about the First Miracle (Jesus Heals a Blind Man at the Pool of Bethsaida)

Mark 8:22–26

5. Read verse 22. What can be determined or assumed about who some people were? (The term some people is used in several versions of the Bible.)

6. Jesus did two things with the man. "And he took the blind man by the hand and led him out of the village" (verse 23). It is probably

obvious why Jesus took him by the hand, but why would He have taken him out of the village?

7. How can one determine that this man had not been born blind?

8. Answer the following about the process used by Jesus:

    a. Why do you think Jesus used a two-step process to heal this blind man?
    b. Could it be that part of the reason for the two-step process was, it was a particularly difficult miracle for Him to perform? Explain your answer.

9. Why do you think Jesus said to the man, "Do not even enter the village?" The NLT says it differently from the ESV: "Don't go back into the village on your way home." Part of the challenge of the question is to determine what village Jesus referred to.

Questions about the Second Miracle (Jesus Heals a Man Blind Since Birth)

John 9:1–16

10. What does the title *rabbi* mean, and why was it so fitting that Jesus would be called that?

11. In John 9:4, Jesus says, "We must work the works of him who sent me while it is day; night is coming, when no one can work." These words are full of teaching which can be better understood by answering the following questions:

a. Why did Jesus the word we in the first part of the sentence and then change to the word me further on in the same sentence?
b. What do you think the work is that Jesus mentioned?
c. What is the day and what is the night?
d. What does it mean when Jesus said that "no one can work"?

12. Herbert Lockyer says that this miracle has five sections.[62] Look at each of them below and answer the question or questions associated with each.

   a. *The plight of the blind man.* While being blind is certainly reason enough to be concerned for another human being, is there anything else that stands out about this particular blind man? You may find this in the verses, or you may see something that is written between the lines. Besides the verses for this miracle and your own thoughts, you may want to use John 9:32 to help with the answer.
   b. *The question of the disciples*

      i. Why would the disciples have asked the question, "Rabbi, who sinned, this man or his parents?" See if you can find a verse(s) in the Old Testament that would explain why they asked the question.
      ii. Why can it be assumed that it was highly unlikely, even impossible, that the first part of their question had no merit?

[62] Lockyer, "The Miracle of the Man Born Blind," 220–223.

c. *The answer of Jesus.* How can you contrast what is written in Deuteronomy 28:15–22 with what Jesus said in John 9:3?
d. *The care of the blind beggar.* There are at least two unusual features of the healing of this blind man that are unique. You can find one of those points by looking at Mark 8:22 from the first miracle in the lesson, and you can find the other unique point in John 9:1 from the second miracle. When combined, what message do you get about Jesus?
e. *The division among the Pharisees*

    i. As a result of what Jesus did, there was division within the Pharisees. Reading on a little beyond where the miracle is recorded in John, what was the division that occurred?
    ii. Why would each group of Pharisees argue the way they did?

13. What are you reminded of when Jesus made mud from the earth and applied it to the man's eyes?

Summary Questions Based on Both Miracles

14. Although both men were blind and illness entered the world because of Adam and Eve, what is the great message in both miracles?

15. How did these miracles affect the following:

    a. the one who performed the miracles
    b. the blind men on whom the miracles were performed

c. the ones who witnessed the miracle of the man born blind (John 9:13–16)

16. Read Paul's statement in 1 Corinthians 13:12 and then compare and contrast it with the quote below. What is the most meaningful message you get from either or both statements?

Our Lord's method certainly illustrates the progressive step in our spiritual enlightenment. At first, we do not see clearly; much of the old blindness remains; but with fuller faith and complete obedience, clarity of vision comes from Him who is not only the Author of our faith but also its Finisher.[63]

[63] Lockyer, "The Miracle of the Bethsaida Blind Man," 212.

LESSON 24
Jesus Casts Out a Demon from a Boy

As you survey your life in the years that you have lived and continue to survey your life going forward from the present, do you see a straight line with no bumps or difficulties or highs and lows? Has your life just been one big happy journey from birth to today? Or do you see a lifeline that looks more like a roller coaster with some very definite highs and some just as definite lows? Are there times when you are creeping along and other times when you are going full speed ahead with your arms in the air and yelling ecstatically when you head downhill and back to another low?

Now turn your eyes toward Jesus. Were all His days bowls of cherries or did He just get the pits on occasion? Did He have a calm and collected life all the time, or did He have the highs and lows just like people do today? If He had highs and lows, when did He experience them? And perhaps most important of all, how did He deal with them? There is no need to look any further than the miracles He performed to get an idea of what His life was like on a daily basis.

Start with the miracle that involved Jesus casting evil spirits out of a demoniac and into a herd of pigs. With that story, one sees almost at once that Jesus had saved the demoniac and gotten rid of the evil spirits that were indwelling him. That had to feel great for the demoniac, the disciples, and even Jesus. But was that the case for everyone? No! The pig herders and the people who owned the pigs put much more emphasis on lost revenue and no emphasis on the healing of a man who had been plagued for years by demons. They disliked what Jesus had done so much that they drove Him out of the community! In this case, the high that Jesus may have felt was quickly replaced by a low caused by uncaring people who saw only the ruination of their ability to earn money.

In another instance, look back at what Jesus did when He healed the blind men—one born blind and one who became blind at some point in his life. The man born blind was healed, and "Never since the world began has it been heard that anyone opened the eyes of a man born blind" (John 9:32). The one who had not been born blind was healed just as quickly, and Jesus demonstrated who He was and is and what He could and can do for those in need. Nonetheless, many of the Pharisees decided that Jesus was doing these works by the power of the devil. Here the high came in the healing while the low came when His own people turned their backs on Him in disbelief.

Outside the miracles, consider the high that Jesus must have felt when He dined with the disciples for the last time on what has become known as Maundy Thursday. He was able to demonstrate to them with His action that their role, going forward, was to be servants to others. This must have been a time of great intimacy with those He loved the most, but a great low in the form of betrayal that was not far away. Although He knew this betrayal was about to take place, it still had to happen to fulfill prophecy, and it was going to be done by one of the twelve men of His inner circle. Soon Judas would leave the Last Supper and in the Garden of Gethsemane, supply the Jews and the Romans with what they needed to arrest Jesus. He was hurt by this betrayal, but He was hurt more because of the one who had betrayed Him.

How did Jesus deal with the highs and lows in His life? There was only one way: He went to His Father in heaven both in thanksgiving and in supplication. He found His strength in God who sent Him to earth, in God who charged Him with His mission, and in God who allowed His precious Son to be crucified and killed. If Jesus did that, shouldn't believers today also do it in both our high times and our low times? If it was a good enough thing to do for Messiah, the Savior of the world, surely it is good enough for all Christians!

STUDY GUIDE

If we are to rescue the perishing, we must be found where they are.[64]

Opening Questions

1. As you review the statement above, name one or more ways the following "were found where the perishing were." You may give examples of success or failure on the parts of each of them. (As an example, if Moses were on the list, you might say he was in exile when the Lord decided to call His people out of slavery. Then you might give a little information on what that looked like.)

    a. Elijah
    b. Stephen

[64] Lockyer, "The Miracle of the Demonic Boy," 216.

   c. Paul
   d. Jesus

2. If you were asked to identify where the devil/demons are at work in our society today, what might you point to and why?

3. Can you think of a situation in the Bible where a person overcame an issue or problem by knowing that faith in God is the answer to whatever problem that person might have been experiencing? Consider both the Old and New Testaments. Give the book, chapter, and verse or verses, and tell a little about the situation.

4. Provide a verse or verses that you call on when you struggle with the down moments in your life.

Questions Leading Up to the Miracles

5. The opening thoughts on the first page of this lesson dealt with the concept of highs and lows and some highs and lows that Jesus had. What high had Jesus just experienced that may have been the highest of His life on earth? Identify the event, give a brief synopsis of it, and explain what its greater meaning was/is. (See Mark 9:1–13.)

6. Mark 9:14 reads "And when they came to the disciples, they saw a great crowd around them, and scribes arguing with them." To what people do the following words in this verse apply:

   a. they
   b. disciples
   c. scribes

7. What was it that caused the frenzy of the crowd and the arguing that was going on?

Questions about Miracle

Mark 9:14–29 (also Matthew 17:14–21, Luke 9:37–43)

8. What were the symptoms demonstrated by the boy when the unclean spirit had control? (You may have to look at the story in all three Gospels where this miracle appears.)

9. Why was the father of the boy concerned about what had or had not happened to his son?

10. In verse 19 Jesus says, "O faithless generation, how long am I to be with you? How long am I to bear with you?"

    a. To whom was Jesus speaking when He said, "O faithless generation"? (There are at least two groups of people to whom this may refer.) Explain your answer.
    b. Why do you think Jesus seemed to be frustrated, perhaps even angry?

11. Since the disciples had not been able to heal the boy, why do you think the people brought the boy to Jesus?

12. Why do you think the evil spirit did what it did in verse 20?

13. What was the purpose behind Jesus asking, "How long has this been happening to him?"

14. Herbert Lockyer in *All the Miracles of the Bible* summarizes this miracle into four distinct parts.[65] Look at each of those below and answer the questions associated with each:

    a. *The distressed father*

        i. When you read the Matthew account of this miracle, what is the very first thing you notice about the father, and why do you think he responded as he did? (See Matthew 17:14.)
        ii. Returning to Mark's account (and this is well said in *The Message*), what is it that the father said to Jesus, and why did Jesus respond almost indignantly to the man (and to the crowd)?
        iii. What positive effect did what Jesus said have on the father? What does this indicate about the father of the boy?

    b. *The demented boy.* What do you learn about the boy with the unclean spirit that shows that the boy's problem was not just a bother but was much more serious than that?
    c. *The omnipotent Christ.* In what one or more ways do you see the omnipotence of Christ being demonstrated in this miracle?
    d. *The impotent disciples.* This one may be puzzling. Why do you think Lockyer saw the disciples as impotent, and regardless of the reason do you think that was justified?

---

[65] Lockyer, 216–218.

Summary Questions

15. After reading verses 28 and 29 answer the following:

    a. Why did the disciples ask Jesus privately about why they failed to cast out the demon?
    b. What did Jesus mean when He said, "This kind cannot be driven out by anything but prayer"?
    c. What does this tell you about the disciples and what they didn't understand?

16. Herbert Lockyer speaks of the power of faith as being both vicarious and victorious. What do you think he means by saying that about faith's power?

17. Of all the points made in this miracle, what do you see as the most important one that Mark was trying to get across?

18. How do you feel about the statement below? What does it mean? Does the author of the statement have a grasp on what the church should do? (Answer any one or all of those questions.)

It is still a pain and a wound to Christ to see His church stand impotent and depressed amidst the woes she might cure, if only she could stir up the power within her.[66]

---

[66] Lockyer, 217.

LESSON 25

The Miracle of the Coin in the Fish's Mouth

In the very first lesson in this study of the miracles of Jesus, this statement was made: "There are a couple of very important points to note about Christ regarding the miracles He performed. First, He never used His power in performing miracles for His own safety and aggrandizement. Second, He never worked a single miracle on His own behalf. Enriching others, He elected to remain impoverished. This may be one of the more fascinating aspects of the miracles of Jesus because His human side might want some of the glory for what He did. However, as He told us, He came to do what we are expected to do—serve others—and it is difficult to have a true servant's heart if we are looking for some sort of glory for ourselves." With this statement in mind, it is fitting to look at how that has held true through some of the miracles studied thus far.

1. When Jesus turned water into wine, He kept a wedding host from embarrassment.
2. In the first miracle dealing with fish, Peter began his ministry of "catching men."

3. When He healed the centurion's servant, He showed He was here for both Jews and Gentiles.
4. In raising the widow's son, Jesus gave the woman hope for the future.
5. Calming the sea gave the disciples one more glimpse of who Jesus truly was.
6. Feeding the 4,000 and the 5,000 cared for people's basic needs.
7. When He healed two blind men, Jesus gave two men the blessing of sight.

These are just a few of the miracles in this study, and there is no knowledge of how many more miracles He performed. How many more people did He heal while He was on earth? How many more miracles were used specifically to help the twelve disciples know who He really was? How many more people were restored to full life with just the touch of His hand? The miracles that are recorded are the miracles that God wanted to be known, and these are sufficient for believers to get a feel for the power, love, mercy, and grace of the Savior and Lord Jesus Christ.

Jesus's miracles, as amazing as they were, teach something more than just the surface value of the supernatural acts of the Lord. Each of the miracles was designed to teach the disciples, the people who witnessed the miracles, and Christians today valuable lessons. For instance, the last miracle in the seven listed above taught the truth of physical healing, but more importantly, it taught the truth of spiritual healing. People have physical sight to see the world around them, but they need spiritual sight to see the wonder of the truth of God's Holy Word. It is through spiritual sight that man is led to God to accept His grace to inherit eternal life.

This lesson takes a peculiar twist because it negates some of the statements made in the introduction. This lesson will take a different kind of thinking to really discover what is going on. Hopefully, with prayer and the leading of the Holy Spirit, the meaning of this lesson's miracle and the reason Jesus performed it will become less ambiguous and more demonstrative of who Jesus was and is and why He did the things he did while on earth.

He never spoke a word that did not have meaning. He never performed a miracle that did not have a much deeper implication. He never told a parable whose meaning was hidden from those who had ears to hear. Just as the word was true then, it is just as true today. Take His words and let the Holy Spirit write them on your heart. You will never regret it today or in the future when believers are taken home to be with Him forever!

STUDY GUIDE

Abiding in Capernaum, probably in the home of Peter, Jesus spent His time instructing His disciples in his coming death and resurrection. He wanted His sayings to sink down into their hearts ... as yet they did not fully understand all that Jesus was to accomplish by His passion.[67]

Opening Questions

1. Read Matthew 16:21, 17:22–23, and 20:17–19.

   a. What are the major points of these three passages of scripture? You may have to piece together all the

[67] Lockyer, "The Miracle of the Coin in the Fish's Mouth," 218.

important ones by consolidating the points made in the three passages.

b. Why do you think the disciples failed to understand what Jesus was telling them?

c. *Challenge.* Answer the following:

    i. Find one or more Old Testament passages that prophesied part or all of what Jesus told the disciples.

    ii. Why should they have known what the Old Testament taught?

    iii. Why might they not have known as much as they should? (See Matthew 9:36.)

d. With regard to the Christian faith, what aspect of the faith do you think today's believers have the most trouble grasping? Answer from a general and/or a personal point of view.

2. As He wrapped up His earthly ministry, why was it so important for Jesus to teach the disciples about what would take place in the days ahead? Give a verse or verses that validate your answer.

3. Name two or three things they finally learned that can be demonstrated by what they did or by what was done to them. (This question looks to the future.)

Questions Leading Up to the Miracle

4. Regarding what had taken place immediately preceding the miracle (Matthew 17:22–23), answer the following:

a. What had taken place?
b. Why were the disciples greatly distressed as Matthew 17:23 says?
c. If they had really been paying attention to Jesus's words, how should they have felt about what He told them and why?

Questions about the Miracle

Matthew 17:24–27

5. It is interesting to note that this miracle is recorded only in the book of Matthew. Why do you think that Matthew might have been the logical one to have written about what took place?

6. Why were so many Jewish people angry with tax collectors such as Matthew and Zacchaeus?

7. Read Matthew 22:15–22. Using those verses and other reference materials, answer the following questions:

    a. What is the difference between the two taxes that are talked about? (You can find out about one of the taxes in Exodus 30:11–16. The other type of tax can be found in Matthew 22:15–22.)
    b. Who was charged with collecting each of the two kinds of taxes?
    c. Why did one kind of tax make the Jews mad, and why did the other kind of tax not make them mad?
    d. Why would the Jews have had to pay one of the taxes while the other was less obligatory?

8. Examine the conversation between Jesus and Peter as outlined below and give your impressions of what each part of the conversation is talking about. This is the most important part of the miracle.

    a. Jesus said, "What do you think, Simon? From whom do kings of the earth take toll or tax? From their sons or from others?"
    b. Peter said, "From others."
    c. Jesus said, "Then the sons are free."

9. From a purely earthly and practical standpoint, why was it that Jesus depended on Peter finding a coin in a fish's mouth to pay the tax referenced in this miracle?

10. What did Jesus speak about in verse 27?

Summary Questions

11. Some claim there are no less than five points about this miracle making it unique when compared to other miracles. What do you see that is unique in the miracle about the coin in a fish's mouth?

12. What do you think this miracle affirms about the Lord?

13. What does this miracle tell you about the following:

    a. Jesus
    b. those wanting to collect the temple tax
    c. the disciples
    d. believers today

14. How does Romans 12:18 reflect the lesson taught by this miracle?

15. Does this miracle help you understand and/or feel more or less accepting of the taxes today that must be paid to the government at all levels? Why or why not?

LESSON 26

Jesus Heals a Mute Demon-Possessed Man

There appears to be a pattern that most miracles follow regardless of what the miracle itself might be. While this may not hold true to form in each one, the pattern looks like the following:

1. Something significant happened right before a miracle;
2. Jesus recognized the need that an individual or group of people had;
3. Jesus determined if the person or persons had faith;
4. Once He knew that faith was present, the person was, or people were, healed or saved;
5. The person or persons went away rejoicing, and
6. A crowd of people not directly involved with the miracle were astonished and affected by it.

And of course, as with everything Jesus did, there were often His detractors (mainly the Jewish leadership) present to pounce on Him when they thought or hoped He would do or say something that was seen as blasphemous. In the miracle of the coin in the fish's mouth, the pattern changed a little because it is not known for certain that the miracle was fulfilled. Since Jesus gave Peter direct instructions, one can assume that Peter complied with the wishes of his rabbi Jesus, but there is no hard written evidence that it occurred. In the miracle of this lesson, the steps really turn the pattern upside down.

Compare the numbered bullets outlined above with the three points below and note what causes the miracle in Luke 11:14 to be different than most, if not all, of the miracles studied thus far:

> (2) Jesus had not recognized the need of a person.
> (3) There is no record that Jesus found the person had faith.
> (5) While the man spoke, there is no mention that he went away rejoicing.

However, three points do follow the pattern:

> (1) Something significant had happened right before the miracle.
> (4) The person was healed.
> (6) The crowd marveled at what had taken place.

The Holy Spirit inspired Luke to provide limited information about the miracle and the specific events leading up to it yet provided information about what happened after the miracle was performed. Why would the Spirit do that? Christians certainly cannot think as God does or do what He does (Isaiah 55:8–9), but they do know that many of the things God does do not necessarily always make sense to Christians. Why were Adam and Eve given a choice to sin or not to sin? Why did Jacob's mother work with him to steal the birthright of Jacob's brother? Why was David a man after God's own heart even if he committed murder and adultery?

STUDY GUIDE

In Luke, the terms demon and demons occur 16 times and evil spirit(s) (unclean spirit[s] in KJV) occurs 8 times. Jesus always had authority over the demons—a sign of His messianic power (7:21; 13:32). The demons themselves recognized that authority (4:31–41; 8:28–31), and Jesus' enemies did too (11:14–26). Jesus gave others power over demons (9:1), and His authority over demons amazed the crowds (4:36; 9:42–43).[68]

Opening Questions

1. What do Matthew 9:32–34, 12:22–24, and Luke 11:14–16 have in common?

2. Why did the people who made the accusation in each of the verses in question 1 above do so?

3. See what you can find out about Beelzebul/Beelzebub such as meaning, origin, and whatever other facts you find that are interesting. The two spellings have different meanings.

Questions about the Miracle

Luke 11:14–23

4. Review the miracle by answering the following questions:

    a. What was the role of Jesus in this miracle?

[68] Walvoord and Zuck, "Jesus accused of demonic power," 235.

   b. What was the problem the healed man had before Jesus came to him?
   c. What do you learn from the man speaking right after the cure?
   d. What was the reaction of the people who saw the miracle performed?

5. Read verses 15 and 16, then answer the following:

   a. What were the people really saying about Jesus in verse 15?
   b. Verse 16 seems straightforward, but what were the others really doing?

6. Read Mark 3:28–29. Provide your understanding of what it means to blaspheme against the Holy Spirit.

7. How do the answers in question 5 above correspond with blaspheming the Holy Spirit?

8. Is a true Christian capable of blaspheming the Holy Spirit today? Whether your answer is yes or no, explain.

9. Consider the two sides taken by the people who witnessed the miracle (Luke 11:15–16).

   a. What were the two sides?
   b. *Challenge.* What did the two sides not take into consideration?

10. Rather than detracting from the miracle, arguing among themselves, and seeking more answers, what should the people have done based on the knowledge they had about Jesus's ministry?

11. As believers, what should be done based on knowledge about Jesus's ministry?

12. The crux of the aftermath of the miracle is captured in Luke 11:17–22. Read those verses several times and using different versions of the Bible, answer the following.

    a. What is the message about a kingdom divided against itself?
    b. Why does Jesus point out that Satan may be divided against himself?
    c. Jesus asked, "If I cast out demons by Beelzebul, by whom do your sons cast them out?" What was Jesus talking about with that question?
    d. Who is it that will be your judges and why?
    e. Jesus said in verse 20, "But if it is by the finger of God that I cast out demons, then the kingdom of God has come upon you." This statement is in the present tense. What do you think that means? (The meaning has been argued over the years by great theologians!)
    f. What do verses 21 and 22 mean?

13. Who was Jesus addressing in verse 23, and why did He make the statement He made in that verse, particularly the last part of the verse, "Whoever does not gather with me scatters"?

14. Provide a verse in the Old or New Testament that justifies what Jesus said in verse 23.

15. What does this statement say to you, "We can reject Jesus, but to doubt his miracles is to question not only him but also, curiously enough, his opponents"?[69]

Summary Questions

In other miracle stories, considerable attention is given to the occasion, setting, and nature of the miracle. In some texts, such detail spans thirteen verses (Mark 5:1–13). But in Luke 11:14–23 all these elements appear in a single verse.[70]

16. Referencing the quote above, the miracle takes up one verse and the reaction to the miracle takes up the rest of the passage. What is significant about that?

17. What three arguments do you see regarding Jesus's challenge to the people?

[69] "Why Miracles?," accessed March 1, 2019, https://www.biblegateway.com/resources/ivp-nt/Why-miracles.

[70] "Miracles," https://www.biblegateway.com/resources/encyclopedia-of-the-bible/Miracles.

LESSON 27
Jesus Heals a Crippled Woman

Long-suffering—what is it all about? Very simply put, long-suffering means to suffer long! One who is long-suffering is said to have a long fuse and patiently forbears. It is an attribute that is associated with mercy in 1 Peter 3:20 and hope in 1 Thessalonians 1:3. The long-suffering person does not surrender to circumstances or succumb to trial. While those two verses speak to the attribute, the Bible is replete with stories of various people who fit the very definition of the word.

The first clear example of being long-suffering is the story of Noah, which resulted in the Noahic covenant with the Lord. Noah did what the Lord told him to do even though it took years to complete the ark, and Noah and his family must have suffered as a result of being ridiculed while they were building what God had told Noah to build. But because of what he was willing to do, his family became the ones who repopulated all the earth.

Abram (Abraham) and Sarai (Sarah) are two of the better-known examples of long-suffering because they had to wait for a number of years between God's promise of a son and the actual birth, and they had to trust God completely because they were well up in years when the promised child Isaac was born. At one point, they tried to push things along with the birth of Ishmael through a concubine, but they found out that was not God's way.

There are other stories in the Old Testament that show long-suffering in God's people such as Jacob waiting to marry Rachel, the one he loved; David waiting to become king of Israel while Saul was still alive; Daniel being in captivity for most of his adult life but never straying from God; Nehemiah biding his time in exile until he was able to go to Jerusalem and rebuild the city's wall; and all the prophets, who for the most part, never saw the results of their work.

Moving into the New Testament there are several stories that show the long-suffering of people who trusted God. To name a few, consider the following:

- Zachariah and Elizabeth waited until late in life to have a son, John the Baptist;
- Simon waited for the arrival of the Messiah to see the promise of God;
- Anna spent all her time in the temple worshipping and getting to know God better, and
- John, the disciple, spent many years in exile because of his love for the Lord.

Though not an exhaustive list by any means, these are all notable examples of people who were willing to be patient and wait for what God promised. However, their examples of long-suffering pale in comparison to one other person in the Bible—God, the creator of all things! He is an example of patience and endurance. He demonstrates what long-suffering truly is because He wants nothing more than for all people to come to Him. The website gotquestions.org says it best, "The ultimate example of God's longsuffering is His waiting for individuals to respond in faith to Jesus Christ. God is not willing that any should perish but that all should come to repentance (2 Peter 3:9)."[71]

STUDY GUIDE

God's Word Speaks

Romans 12:12 is a perfect verse for a lesson such as this, "Rejoice in hope, be patient in tribulation, be constant in prayer." Just as the woman in the miracle in this lesson, Christians can rejoice in the fact that hope is with every believer today, that believers are learning to be patient as they deal with the new normal, and that all believers need to be in prayer constantly for God's hand to rule and reign as only He can.

Opening Questions

1. In his book, *All the Miracles of the Bible,* Herbert Lockyer states, "Faith, not works of ceremonial observance, is the standing principle of blessing from God."[72]

    a. Provide a verse(s) from the Old Testament that says very much the same as the quote from Lockyer. Give the book, chapter, and verse(s).
    b. Where do you find the principle of what Lockyer said (1) at work in society today and (2) not at work in society today?

---

[71] "What does the Bible mean by longsuffering?," https://www.gotquestions.org/Bible-longsuffering.html.

[72] Lockyer, "The Miracle of the Infirm Woman," 224.

   c. How does your church, or a church you have known in the past, adhere to the principle?

2. *Challenge.* How did the following, more obscure people in the Old Testament, show this principle?

   a. Mordecai
   b. Jethro (Reuel or Hobab)
   c. Shiphrah and Puah

3. What phrase or variation of the phrase defined every king of Judah and Israel after Solomon, and what does that tell you about individual kings and about God? (The phrase can be found at the end of the reign of each of the kings.)

Questions Leading Up to the Miracle

4. Luke 13:10 states, "He [Jesus] was teaching in one of the synagogues." Define what the word *synagogue* means. See what you can find out about the number of synagogues that might have been in a town or city at that time in history.

5. What is the primary reason or reasons that Jesus chose to teach in the synagogues as one part of His ministry?

Questions about the Miracle

Luke 13:10–17

6. Luke is the only Gospel that records this miracle. What one or more reasons can you think of that made him the right one to write about the woman?

7. While the *ESV* refers to a disabling spirit, what do other translations say about the condition that affected this woman?

8. This woman had suffered for eighteen years.

    a. Think back over the miracle lessons up to this point and list any other of those healed who had a specific time reference.
    b. Why do you think it is important to know the number of years she had suffered?
    c. How would this have limited her over the time she was disabled?

9. While it is not known for sure, there are at least a couple of points in this miracle that might lead to believing that the woman was a follower of the God of the Jews. What are those points, and do you find any other points as you read this story in other translations of the Bible?

10. What do you learn about Jesus in verse 12? There may be more than one thing.

11. Who was it that challenged Jesus, and in review from a previous lesson, what was this person responsible for because of his role? Why is it significant to know that?

12. Lockyer uses the term *caviling ruler* to describe the head of the synagogue.[73] What does this term mean? Is this a fitting term to use? Why or why not?

13. One modifier used to describe the synagogue ruler is indignant. What does that word mean to you, and why was it inappropriate for him to be indignant about what Jesus was doing?

14. As you read verse 14, still in reference to the synagogue ruler, what does he do that is unusual, even rude when speaking to Jesus, and what does that say about the ruler?

15. What does this statement from verse 14 say about the synagogue ruler? "There are six days in which work ought to be done. Come on those days and be healed, not on the Sabbath day"?

16. Mark 2:27 says, "And he [Jesus] said to them, 'The sabbath was made for man, not man for the Sabbath.'" What does this statement mean?

17. Give your own synopsis of why Jesus called the people hypocrites. To whom was this name directed?

---

[73] Lockyer, 223.

Summary Questions

18. What was the result of this miracle for Jesus, for Jesus's enemies, and for the people who saw it?

19. Herbert Lockyer says, "By the working of so many miracles on this day [the Sabbath], He consecrated it to the purposes of His Gospel." What does that statement mean to you?

20. How is this miracle representative of man's spiritual condition? You may want to use Psalm 40:12 to help with your answer.

21. Read the quote below. What does it mean when it says, "It [endurance] is necessary to spread the Gospel?"

In the Bible, believers are called to endure for a purpose. Endurance is necessary to overcome the trials of this life. It is necessary to spread the Gospel. It is important because if the believer endures to the end, there is glory with the Savior in eternity.[74]

---

[74] "In the Bible believers are with the Savior in eternity," accessed March 1, 2019, https://www.crosswalk.com/faith/spiritual-life/this-too-shall-pass-is-in-the-bible-isnt.it.html.

LESSON 28
Jesus Heals a Man with Dropsy

In 2020 and 2021 anyone who watched a television news show or listened to the news on radio stations heard little but reporting on COVID-19 and the many ways it was talked about and spun. COVID-19 dominated the news as nothing quite like it had been seen or heard on the news since 911. The biggest problem with the COVID-19 news was that not much more was known after tuning into the news. What was known was more from the standpoint of a particular network or cable station and their take on what was really happening.

That, in and of itself, was bad enough, but the unintended consequences—and the intended ones—were the anxiety, fear, and panic that was setting in across the nation and around the world. Why was that? It was because COVID-19 was something that no one could control. Some thought the panic was worse than the disease, and others noted that lines at supermarkets were a result of panic even though the supply chain was working quite well for many of the products that were needed.

So what does that virus have to do with what was going on in the time of Jesus or before? While there are certainly no direct parallels, there are some events and diseases that might come close. Some are in the Old Testament, and some are in the New Testament. Some of them were allowed to happen because of the sins of God's people against Yahweh while others did not relate to sin at all. Both of those need to be looked at a little more closely.

Events. The most obvious event that church-going people all learned about from the earliest days of Sunday school is the series of plagues that fell on the Egyptians because of Pharaoh's obstinance in keeping God's people in slavery. There were ten plagues in all, and the most horrific plague occurred when the firstborn of all those in Egypt, except those of Jewish households with blood on their doorposts, died in the night.

Diseases. The disease of leprosy in both the Old Testament and the New Testament was mortifying. It was not a matter of the disease killing people, which it did, as much as it was the way it ostracized people and kept them out of all aspects of Jewish society from their families to their faith. Other diseases, some of which have been studied in other miracles, were deafness, muteness, blindness, bleeding issues, and paralysis.

Disease and all other evil entered life because of Adam and Eve, and disease and all sorts of evil things continue today because of that original sin. For some people, events make them stronger while other people fall under the weight of the health burden they face. Many people suffer physically at some point, and all people most likely suffer spiritually at some time in their lives. But whether it was in Old Testament times, New Testament times, or today, there is one thing that was as sure then as it is now: God can and will restore people if they lean on Him and His mercy. It may not be physical healing in this life, but it is known, for certain, that for those in Christ Jesus, all spiritual suffering and tears and woes will be wiped away forever when He returns!

STUDY GUIDE

During His ministry on earth, Jesus was not the kind of person who turned down an invitation. He went to the homes of tax collectors and other sinners, and he went to the homes of Pharisees and other righteous people. He went to wedding feasts, and He ate with His disciples by the seaside. He ate with friends, and He ate with foes. He ate with the twelve disciples before His arrest, and He even broke bread with two of them on the evening when He had just been resurrected from the dead.

Opening Questions

1. If someone asked you to describe the difference between knowing about Jesus and knowing Jesus, what would you tell them?

2. Keeping the first question in mind answer the following:

    a. What verse(s) would you direct a person to if they wanted to know Jesus?
    b. Did the Jewish leadership (Pharisees, Sadducees, Sanhedrin, etc.) know Jesus or did they know about Jesus? Explain your answer.
    c. Give a verse or verses that demonstrate that someone wanted to know about Jesus.

Questions Leading Up to the Miracle

3. The last lesson was about a woman who had been disabled for eighteen years (Luke 13:10–17). According to the book of

Luke, three events happened between that miracle and the miracle being studied in this lesson—"Healing of the Man with Dropsy." Beginning with Luke 13:18, identify those three events and give a brief synopsis of what each event was about. If you can, explain how the events should affect believers today.

a. first event
b. second event
c. third event

4. How many miracles were performed by Jesus on the Sabbath, and what were they (just a title for each)?

5. Why do you think He chose to perform miracles on the Sabbath when He knew that He would make enemies of those who wanted to hurt Him?

6. Skim Luke 11:39–52 and give an overview of what Jesus was doing in those verses.

Questions about the Miracle

Luke 14:1–6

7. It is safe to assume that Jesus was invited to the home of the Pharisee mentioned in these verses.

    a. Why do you think one of the Jewish leaders would have invited Jesus to eat with him?
    b. Why do you think Jesus accepted the invitation?
    c. What in Luke 14:1 reveals that Jesus was on enemy ground?

8. The term *dropsy* may be relatively unknown. What does it mean in terms of disease today, and how would it have disabled the man?

9. Look back at Luke 13:14–15 and Luke 14:3. What difference do you see in the discourses Jesus and the Pharisees had in the verses?

10. Why do you think the Jewish leaders remained silent after Jesus asked His question in Luke 14:3?

11. Jesus asked the question in verse 3. Then in verse 4, the Pharisees remained silent and Jesus healed the man. Then Jesus made a statement to the Pharisees in verse 5. Compare Jesus's statement here to His statement in Luke 13:15. How did Jesus elevate the stakes in this miracle versus the previous one? Explain why that was important.

12. What was the Jewish leadership saying about their personal values?

Summary Questions

13. *The Bible Exposition Commentary* states the following: "There is a big difference between protecting God's truth and promoting man's tradition."[75]

    a. Where do you see promoting man's tradition as opposed to protecting God's truth in churches or in society today?

[75] Wiersbe, "The Pharisees: False Piety," https://www.logos.com.

   b. When man's traditions supersede God's truth, how is the Gospel diluted and weakened?
   c. What should you do if you see that happening in churches today?

14. How did this miracle affect the following:

   a. the one who performed the miracle
   b. the ones who witnessed the miracle
   c. the ones who study the miracle today

15. Based on this miracle, how can believers best be prepared to silence those who are critical of the Word of God and Jesus? Identify at least one verse in the New Testament that speaks directly to this.

16. Read the quote below. In what ways do His followers today "sit at the table with Jesus" and not know Him?

They were sitting at the table with God manifested in flesh, and they "watched Him, yet they were so blinded that they knew Him not.[76]

[76] Lockyer, "The Miracle of the Dropsical Man," 225.

LESSON 29
Jesus Heals Ten Lepers

America is blessed in so many ways—ways too numerous to count. The nation has freedoms that are unparalleled in the world; the economy is typically one of the most robust anywhere; public education, while lacking in some areas, is still superior to that of many other countries; and the United States has medical and dental care that has few equals in other countries of the world.

At the same time, people often complain that they do not have this, or they do not have that, and during the 2020–2022 COVID-19 pandemic, people were frustrated that they could not just get in their cars and go out and do the things they had always done. With 9/11 on September 11, 2001, there were restrictions, but they were short-lived, and even though people today still experience some of the effects and restrictions relating to that event, life quickly got back to as normal as it could.

After 9/11 you may recall the tremendous rebirth of people returning to places of worship because of those terrible terrorist actions, and you may also recall how brief that rebirth was. It was as if people in America had the attention span of a two-year-old because within a few weeks after the deadliest terrorist event in the history of the United States, people returned to their normal lives for the most part. In addition, America has been on a downhill moral slide ever since which shows God is even further out of Americans' lives than before 9/11.

However, the world has always been a decadent place even in the time when Paul was starting the church all over Asia. There was so much evil in cities like Corinth that some of the believers were not sure what was okay and what was not in relation to what was expected of them as Christians. Because of that, some of the new believers were setting examples that were not what Christ intended Christians to be. But Paul fought the battle using the truth, and many of those early Christians came around to being all that was expected of them in their new faith.

While Christians try to be faithful believers and try to love the Lord with all their hearts, all still sin and fall short of God's standards. However, because of what Christ did on the cross for all believers, all sins are forgiven—sins of the past, the present, and the future. Forgiveness does not mean believers can sin more because they can, but regardless, people will continue to sin because of the sin nature that has been imparted to all humanity by what Adam and Eve did in the Garden of Eden. Yet even with the knowledge of what Christ did on the cross, devout Christians often forget to give thanks for the forgiveness which they have received.

Psalm 86:12–13 should be a daily reading because it instructs believers how to live, "I give thanks to you, O Lord my God, with my whole heart, and I will glorify your name forever. For great is your steadfast love toward me." When one's life seems to be disintegrating moment by moment, every Christian should be able to find many things for which to thank God.

STUDY GUIDE

God's Word Speaks

Oh, give thanks to the LORD; call upon his name; make known his deeds among the peoples! Sing to him, sing praises to him; tell of all his wondrous works! (Psalm 105:1–2).

Let us intreat God to save us from the dark sin of ingratitude.[77]

Opening Questions

1. Consider some people in the Bible who gave thanksgiving to God. With that in mind say a little bit about each of the following people and why they thanked God. Give information about their thankfulness and what transpired because they were thankful:

    a. Hannah
    b. Ezra
    c. Hezekiah
    d. Daniel

2. The most famous prayer in scripture is the Lord's Prayer. Recite that to yourself and see what is missing from it (reference the opening notes and the first question). Why do you think that is?

[77] Lockyer, "The Miracle of the Ten Lepers," 232.

Questions Leading Up to the Miracle

3. Between Luke 17:10 and Luke 17:11, the events of John 11 occurred.

    a. What was the lesson Jesus taught right before Luke 17:11?
    b. Skim John 11. What were the two main lessons Jesus taught?

4. Luke 17:11 says Jesus was on the way to Jerusalem passing between Samaria and Galilee. Answer the following about that journey.

    a. Find the relative positions of Galilee, Samaria, and Jerusalem in Judea.
    b. *Challenge.* If Jesus was going from Galilee to Jerusalem, why does Luke 17:11 say He was passing along between Samaria and Galilee? That would tend to indicate He was going in the wrong direction. What point was Jesus making by going in the direction he went?

Questions about the Miracle

Luke 17:11–19

5. The *ESV* titles this section of scripture "Jesus Cleanses Ten Lepers." Look at the number ten as the actual number of lepers that approached Jesus or look at the number ten as something more abstract. If abstract, what might the number ten represent?

6. What can you tell about the ten lepers in verses 12 and 13?

7. Verse 12 says the lepers stood at a distance. Was there a specific distance lepers were to stand away from others? (Research in the Bible to help you find an answer.)

8. Jesus said, in verse 14, "Go and show yourselves to the priests."

   a. Why did Jesus tell the lepers to do that?
   b. Using your answer in question 8a above along with Matthew 5:17, what do you discover about Jesus?
   c. The Matthew 5:17 statement was made in the Sermon on the Mount. Why would Jesus have said that so early in His ministry?

9. What do you see as unusual about how the ten lepers were healed?

10. Regarding the ten lepers answer the following:

    a. Why do you think nine of the lepers did not return to praise Jesus and thank Him?
    b. Question 5 asked about the number ten and what it might represent in the abstract. Depending on how you answered that question, what might the number nine represent in the abstract?
    c. Why do you think only one leper returned to praise Jesus and thank Him?
    d. What is remarkable about the one leper that did return? Why was that remarkable?

11. If only one leper returned to thank Jesus, why were all ten lepers healed? What does this tell you about Jesus?

12. What is the significance of the one leper "praising God with a loud voice"?

13. The one who returned was not only healed physically but was also healed spiritually. How can that be determined by what is said in the passage?

14. What were some emotions Jesus might have been feeling based on what He asked in verses 17 and 18?

Summary Questions

15. Can you think of another person in the Bible who was not thankful for something God had done?

16. What might distance, as mentioned in this miracle, represent spiritually?

17. What did this miracle mean or would this miracle have meant for the following:

    a. Jesus
    b. the lepers
    c. believers today

18. The quote below makes several points about thankfulness and gratitude. Choose one point and explain how it affects you in a special way.

We should be thankful because God is worthy of our thanksgiving. It is only right to credit Him for "every good and perfect gift"

He gives (James 1:17). When we are thankful, our focus moves off selfish desires and off the pain of current circumstances. Expressing thankfulness helps us remember that God is in control. Thankfulness, then, is not only appropriate; it is actually healthy and beneficial to us. It reminds us of the bigger picture, that we belong to God, and that we have been blessed with every spiritual blessing (Ephesians 1:3). Truly, we have an abundant life (John 10:10), and gratefulness is fitting.[78]

[78] "What does the Bible say about thankfulness/gratitude?," https://www.gotquestions.org/Bible-thankfulness-gratitude.html.

LESSON 30
Jesus Raises Lazarus from the Dead

Eight people + saints in Jerusalem + Jesus = those who were raised from the dead according to the scriptures. Two of those resurrections stand out today as they have stood out since the early years of the first century AD. These two miracles of resurrection linger in the minds of believers today and will linger in the minds of Christians until Christ returns at which time all chosen people will be resurrected together!

Look first at the eight mentioned in the opening paragraph. Identified by name or by connection to someone, these were the widow of Zarepeth's son, the Shunammite woman's son, a man raised from Elisha's grave, the widow of Nain's son, Jairus's daughter, Lazarus, Tabitha, and Eutychus. For the most part, except for perhaps Lazarus, these were nondescript biblical figures that are in the Word to talk about someone other than the person who was raised from the dead. Certainly, those raised were important to family and friends, but their stories of resurrection could have just as easily been about others and yet have made the same point.

Next, look at the saints in Jerusalem, who though unnamed, take on more importance than the named eight for a reason that is especially important to followers of Christ. These saints, no matter what the number may have been, were emblematic of something much greater than themselves. These had gone before Christ and had been numbered in the family of God because righteousness was imputed to them based on their faith. Why is this important? It's because just as they looked forward to the cross, believers today look back to the cross and are saved in the same way: righteousness has been imputed to believers based on their faith.

Finally, comes the only resurrection that really matters: the resurrection of our Lord and Savior, Jesus Christ, the Messiah! He is Immanuel who came to dwell among us. He is the perfect Lamb of God, and because of that, His sacrifice is sufficient for all who call on His name and believe in Him as the One True God. Because of Him and His death on the cross, believers have forgiveness of all sins, and because of Him and His resurrection, Christians have the assurance of eternal life!

The miracle of this lesson brings special attention to one of the eight, Lazarus and his resurrection from the dead. This is one of the stories in the Bible that is very familiar to Christians and to a lesser extent even those who do not believe. He was a dear friend of Jesus, and the shortest verse in the Bible captures how Jesus felt about Lazarus before raising him from the dead, Jesus wept (John 11:35). As strange as this may seem, those two simple words are followed by both praise and condemnation of the Messiah.

All believers who die in Christ will be resurrected as was Lazarus. However, there is a caveat to that. Those who die in Christ will be raised to live in Christ, never to die again. This is the day Christians long for, but it is also the day that only God knows—not even the Son is aware (Matthew 24:36). Until then, the believer is to watch and wait and be prepared for the return of the Lord. What a wonderful day that will be!

STUDY GUIDE

Opening Questions

1. Earlier lessons refer to John calling the miracles of Jesus signs. To review, why did John use that term rather than calling them miracles or wondrous works?

2. John recorded seven miracles in his Gospel: turning water into wine, healing an official's son, healing a paralytic at Bethesda, feeding the 5,000, walking on water, healing a blind man, and raising Lazarus from the dead. Indicate what you believe was the sign associated with each.

3. Use a commentary, the introduction to this lesson, or any other source document and find out how many people were raised from the dead—in both the Old and New Testaments. Provide the person's name who was resurrected and the name of the person who performed the miracle. If there's more you want to share about one or more of them, please do so.

4. The miracle of Jesus raising Lazarus from the dead took place in Bethany. In reference to the timeline of Jesus's three-year ministry, when did this miracle occur, and what would soon be taking place in Jesus's life?

5. *Challenge. The Bible Exposition Commentary* states there are two locations that are pertinent in the factors leading up to the miracle.[79] See what you can find out about the two by giving

[79] Wiersbe, "The Disciples," https://www.logos.com.

their location, what they were well known for, and how far apart they were.

   a. Bethany
   b. Bethabara

6. Besides being the place where Lazarus, Mary, and Martha lived, what made Bethany an important place for Jesus and His disciples?

Questions Leading Up to the Miracle

John 11:1–37

7. From the very first words of these verses, there are two women identified: Mary and her sister Martha. Each of the sisters was best known for one activity (Luke 10:38–40).

   a. For what activity was Martha best known?
   b. For what activity was Mary best known?

8. Various parts of the Bible may seem unfair from a human perspective (Cain's versus Abel's sacrifice, Jacob getting Esau's birthright, Lot taking the better land from Abraham, etc.). Does anything seem unfair to you about Jesus's treatment of Mary and Martha and what they did (Luke 10:38–42)? Explain your answer.

9. Why do you think the sisters of Lazarus sent this message to Jesus, "Lord, he whom you love is ill"? See John 11:3.

10. "Now Jesus loved Martha and her sister and Lazarus. So when he heard that Lazarus was ill, he stayed two days longer in the place where he was" (John 11:5–6). Does this show intentionality on the part of Jesus, and if so, why did He hold back from going to Bethany?

11. John 11:8–11 lends itself to at least two questions: What did Jesus mean in verses 9–10? Should the disciples have understood what Jesus meant when He said, "Our friend Lazarus has fallen asleep, but I go to awaken him"? Explain your answer.

12. Martha came out to meet Jesus while Mary stayed "seated in the house." Based on what you know about the sisters, is this a surprise to you? Why or why not?

13. Note the interchange between Jesus and Martha in John 11:21–27.

    a. What is positive and negative about Martha's statement in verse 21?
    b. What is it that Martha hoped for from Jesus in verse 22, and why do you think Martha thought that was possible?
    c. There is both hope and disappointment for Martha in verses 23–24. Is the hope or the disappointment the greater of the two? Explain your answer.

14. The book of John records seven famous *I AM* statements made by Jesus. These were especially important statements and were used for a specific purpose by Jesus. Why were the statements

so important and for what purpose did Christ use them? See Exodus 3:13–14 for help with your answer.

15. John 11:28–37 has several points of interest.

    a. Why do you think Mary used the same words as Martha when she greeted Jesus?
    b. What were the mixed reactions of the people with Mary and Martha?

Questions about the Miracle

John 11:38–44

16. Describe the tomb in verse 38. Why were tombs like this in the time of Jesus?

17. What was Martha's big concern about rolling away the stone?

18. What was Jesus's response to Mary?

19. What point or points was Jesus making in verses 41–42?

20. What was the outcome of this miracle, and how did it affect various people who witnessed it?

Summary Questions

21. People think of Jesus in many ways. Some see Him as the means of salvation; others see Him as the mighty Lord in control of all things. Still others see Him as the epitome of love, and still

to others, He may be something completely different than any of these. The important question is what ways do you see Jesus when you think of your relationship with Him?

22. How miracles were accomplished is impossible for the human mind to comprehend, but believers can still wonder about the awesome nature of miracles.

    a. Of all the miracles of Jesus recorded in the Bible—whether studied in these lessons or not—which is the one you would use to demonstrate the incredible power of Jesus to either a fellow believer or a nonbeliever who may be searching for the truth? Explain your answer.
    b. What makes the raising of Lazarus from the dead so unique? After all, other people were raised from the dead in both the Old Testament and the New Testament. (There may be more than one answer to this question.)

The raising of Lazarus from the dead was not our Lord's last miracle before the Cross, but it was certainly His greatest and the one that aroused the most response both from His friends and His enemies. John selected this miracle as the seventh in the series recorded in his book because it was really the climactic miracle of our Lord's earthly ministry. He had raised others from the dead, but Lazarus had been in the grave for four days. It was a miracle that could not be denied or avoided by the Jewish leaders.

LESSON 31
Jesus Heals a Severed Ear

Good things and bad things have a way of coming to an end. Consider the recent pandemic as one that has slowed dramatically if not ended across the world. Is there any way something so devastating as that virus can be seen as both good and bad? For the most part the bad is evident but consider the pandemic from the good side. First, and most importantly, as believers, Christians learned to put their faith in God into action. Even the faithful will never understand why situations such as this occur, but there can be peace when it is understood that God is sovereign from start to finish.

Additionally, people seemed kinder; families spent more time together; God provided a new way to worship; the world stopped to consider what was important, and, as He has done so often throughout history, God showed that His Word is unstoppable. Yes, some people blamed the pandemic on God and turned away from Him, but many more people saw His hand at work even when it looked as if disaster was surely awaiting the world.

Something much more dramatic was happening when the miracle of this lesson took place. Jesus was about to be arrested; He was about to be betrayed by Judas Iscariot, and His disciples really did not understand what was going on. No one other than Christ was in control of these events just as He was in control of all events while He was on earth. This miracle may remind the reader of other times when Jesus was in control whether it was in one of His miracles or in some other part of His ministry.

As an example, in John 8 there is a story about a woman caught in the act of adultery. The punishment for that in the time of Jesus was stoning the woman to death. This woman was brought to the people by some Pharisees who knew the Law of Moses and what was demanded as the punishment for such a woman. The Pharisees asked Jesus about the law hoping to catch Him in an act that would enable them to bring charges against Him. Rather than answering, He bent down and began to write with His finger on the ground. When pressed to respond, Jesus said, "Let him who is without sin among you be the first to throw a stone at her" (John 8:7). Jesus bent down again, began writing, and all the accusers walked away.

That is an example of the power Jesus had over His enemies. It demonstrated the compassion He showed toward one who had no protection. His actions challenged the Pharisees, as well as challenging believers today to be certain to be pure before accusing another of wrongdoing. And He did all this by just speaking seventeen words! He did not get confrontational because He did not need to. He was in total control of that situation just like He showed total control in the miracle to be discussed in this lesson.

Although the woman faced physical death but lived, Jesus faced those in power who would eventually cause His death. However, even though Jesus would soon die, He would gloriously and miraculously rise from the grave. By His sacrifice for all who believe, the faithful are forgiven of all sin—past, present, and future.

Just as He was in control throughout His entire life, Jesus was in total control in His final days on earth. Jesus was in control when the soldiers came to the Garden of Gethsemane. Jesus was in control when Judas betrayed Him with a kiss. Jesus was in control when He was arrested. And Jesus was in control right to the end of His life on earth and His remarkable resurrection three days later. He is in control today, and He will be in control tomorrow including the day on which God sends Him back to take believers home to be with Him!

STUDY GUIDE

His method of conquering force was by submission; violence, by meekness; sin, by the cross. He wins His victories, not by a sword, but by His scars.[80]

Opening Questions

1. Using the quote above, contrast the secular worldview with the Christian worldview.

2. You may think of different things when you hear the word *kiss*. What was the meaning of that word in the time of Jesus? That is, for what was the kiss used?

3. Read 2 Corinthians 10:4 along with this quote from Herbert Lockyer, "It is not right to draw the sword for Christ and His truth." Based on the verse and the quote, what is your opinion about what is said? Is there ever a time when it is right to defend the Word with weaponry? Explain your answer.

[80] Lockyer, "The Miracle of Malchus's Ear," 240.

Questions Leading Up to the Miracle

Luke 22:14–46

4. Read the three accounts of the Last Supper Jesus had with His disciples and pick out those things that are most relevant to what happened that evening in the upper room. Explain what relevance those things have for the Christian faith (Matthew 26:17–29, Mark 14:12–25, Luke 22:7–38).

5. *Challenge.* Jesus had just left the last supper in the upper room and was headed for the Garden of Gethsemane knowing full well what would happen over the next several hours. What do you think might have been going through His head?

6. Read Luke 22:24–30. What do these verses say about the following:

    a. the mindset and attitude of the disciples
    b. the expectations Jesus has for each believer today

7. After Jesus instituted the Lord's Supper in the upper room and before they left for the Mount of Olives, one of the disciples said, "Look, Lord, here are two swords." Jesus's response to that was "It is enough" (Luke 22:38). What did the disciples mean, and what did Jesus's response mean?

8. Where were the Mount of Olives and the Garden of Gethsemane located?

9. Is there anything particularly symbolic about Jesus going to a garden prior to His arrest? Think about a garden at the creation,

a garden at the time of Jesus, and a garden at the coming of the new heaven and the new earth.

10. While in the garden praying, Jesus asked that the cup be removed from Him.

    a. Since He was God incarnate, why would He have prayed that?
    b. Instead of granting Jesus's request, what did God do instead? (See Luke 22:43.)
    c. Are there any other places in scripture where God did the same or a similar thing either for Jesus or for others?

11. Why did Jesus say, "Rise and pray that you may not enter into temptation" to the disciples in Luke 22:46, particularly the second part of the sentence?

Questions about the Miracle

Luke 22:47–53

12. Given that some people who came with the arresting party already knew who Jesus was, why did Judas identify Jesus with a kiss? What can you find out about why this took place?

13. There are three main points in verses 47–53 regarding this event. Using the following verse divisions, what do you think those points are? (They all refer to Jesus and His attributes in some way.)

    a. verses 47–48
    b. verses 49–51

c. verses 52–53

14. In John 18:10, the disciple who cut off the ear of Malchus, the high priest's servant, is identified as Peter. What traits of Peter do you find in this act?

15. Apart from being in opposition to what Jesus wanted, why was it so naïve and even dangerous of Peter to take the action he took with Malchus?

16. Read Matthew 10:34 along with Matthew 26:52. Is there a contradiction in what Jesus said in the two verses? Explain why or why not.

17. What did Jesus say in Matthew 26:53, and why did He not do what He said?

18. How did Jesus's actions embody what He had said earlier in Matthew 5:44?

19. See if you can find a verse or verses in the Bible that prophesied what was happening to Jesus at this time.

Summary Questions

In regard to Peter's defense of his Master, while we applaud the right kind of enthusiasm, we must guard ourselves against the danger of mere impulse.[81]

---

[81] Lockyer, 239.

20. Whether you listed it or not about Peter in question 14 above, could pride have been a motivating factor in what Peter did? Explain your answer.

21. Continuing with Peter, provide the following:

    a. other times he showed strength
    b. other times he showed weakness

22. As you read the quote below think about the history of Christianity. Whose name or names come to mind that would fit the description in the quote?

Church history provides us with the record of those who were willing to perish by the sword rather than defend themselves with it.[82]

---

[82] Lockyer, 240.

LESSON 32
Second Miracle of Catching Fish

This study started with an introduction to the miracles and the miracle of Jesus turning water into wine. This final lesson brings the study to an end with the last miracle performed by Jesus which occurred after His resurrection from the dead and before His ascension to be back with His Father. There were ample lessons learned from the miracles about the way Jesus taught and His message to believers. Throughout His ministry, believers' *faith* in Jesus resulted in *good things*. Here is a recap of some of the miracles and the lessons learned.

There was the woman who had bleeding issues and had spent all her money on doctors who could do nothing for her. In desperation, she got close enough to Jesus to touch His garment, and miraculously she was healed! In the instant she touched His garment and was healed, Jesus called out to identify who had touched him. Although fearing what might happen, she reluctantly fell to the ground and told Jesus that she was the one who had touched the hem of His garment. Instead of being angry, Jesus told her to get up because her faith had made her well. While her earthly life would eventually end, she would be with Jesus forever. Her good thing never ended.

What about the story of the ten lepers and the one of them who returned to thank Jesus for what He had done? He had deep gratitude, and he did not let any time pass before he went back to show that gratitude. Although all ten were healed from the terrible disease, the nine were nowhere to be found after the healing. What a blessing was given to the one who did return! "Rise and go; your faith has made you well." Just like the woman who touched His garment, this one would be with Jesus in paradise eternally. His good thing never ended.

Bartimaeus, the blind beggar, knew that Jesus was in the vicinity where he was, and he called out, "Son of David, have mercy on me." His friends discouraged him and told him to be silent, but he cried out even more. Jesus wanted to see him and asked him, "What do you want me to do for you?" Bartimaeus said, "Let me recover my sight." Jesus responded, "Go your way, your faith has made you well." He walked away from Jesus totally healed—physically and spiritually. His good thing never ended.

How about the Gentile centurion who had a servant, a man whom he loved dearly and on the brink of death when the centurion approached Jesus? The centurion did not feel worthy to have Jesus come under his roof, yet Jesus treated him as if He were a long-lost friend. Jesus healed the man from a distance without going to the official's home. What did Jesus say about this centurion? He said He had never seen such faith in all of Israel even among the Jews. It is safe to say that this man's good thing never ended.

These stories about faith and belief in Jesus, along with many others, are not limited to miracles, and one of the best examples of that is the thief on the cross. The thief on the right recognized who Jesus was, and because he had faith in Jesus, he asked Jesus to remember him when He came into His kingdom. Jesus told the thief that he would be with Him in paradise that very day. While there are no words that mention the thief's faith, it is obvious he had what was required or Jesus would not have told him what He did. While this man may not have been healed physically while on earth, he was healed spiritually. His good thing never ended.

What does the Bible say about faith and its saving properties? Ephesians 2:8 gives a very clear and exact picture, "For by grace you have been saved through faith. And this is not your own doing; it is the gift of God." Think about those words. It is by grace (which He has given to believers) that bestows salvation (which He has given to believers) through faith (which He has given to believers) because it is the greatest gift of God. What does that mean? It means that a believer's good thing will never end! It will go with every believer to paradise to live with Jesus eternally!

STUDY GUIDE

Why did Jesus call so many fishermen to follow Him? For one thing, fishermen are courageous, and Jesus needs brave people to follow Him. They are also dedicated to one thing and cannot easily be distracted. Fishermen do not quit! (We are thinking, of course, of professional fishermen, not idle people on vacation!) They know how to take orders, and they know how to work together.[83]

Opening Questions

1. Verses 30–31 at the end of Chapter 20 of John's Gospel would seem to be a conclusion of John's book. However, he then proceeded to write Chapter 21. Skim Chapter 21:15–25. Why

[83] Wiersbe, "We Are Fishers of Men—Obey Him," https://www.logos.com.

do you think John went on to write this final chapter? (Keep in mind that Peter, James, and John were the closest to Christ.)

2. Christ had been crucified and died. Christ had risen from the grave and appeared to the eleven disciples more than once. What do you think was going on in the minds of the disciples at this point? Explain.

Questions Leading Up to the Miracle

John 21:1–5

3. Why do you think Peter decided to go fishing, and why did some of the other disciples volunteer to go with him?

4. In John 21:2, seven disciples are listed. There are five of them who are named. You will have to determine the names of the other two from what is written about them. What are their names, and what do these disciples have in common?

5. Some Bible scholars believe that it was wrong for Peter to have returned to fishing after the death and resurrection of Jesus. Why would that have been?

Questions about the Miracle

John 21:1–23

6. How successful were the disciples when they went out on this fishing trip?

7. Jesus addressed the disciples in verse 5 as children. "Children, do you have any fish?" (Some translations use the word *children*; another uses the word *friends*, and still another does not use any word of address.) What do you think was meant by the word children in the versions that use it?

8. See if you can find out why an exact number of fish—153—was provided in this miracle. Was there some significance to the number or was there some other more practical reason?

9. Answer the following about verse 7:

    a. Who was the first to recognize Jesus?
    b. See if you can find any information as to why John referred to himself as the disciple whom Jesus loved. Was this a sign of arrogance on the part of John? Why or why not?

10. What happened next that was so typical of Peter?

Summary Questions

11. John 15:5 says, "I am the vine; you are the branches. Whoever abides in me and I in him, he it is that bears much fruit, for apart from me you can do nothing." How do the words "apart from me you can do nothing" support the miracle? You may want to think of this factually or symbolically.

12. Look back at the first miracle of catching fish in Luke 5:1–11 and do a quick comparison of the two miracles—Luke's and John's. What seems to have been the end result of each of the miracles?

13. Symbolically, what do the following two things say about a Christian:

    a. fishing without catching any fish
    b. fishing after Jesus told them to cast the nets to the right side of the boat

Closing Questions from *The Miracles of Jesus*

14. As you think back over the miracles studied, which of the miracles has resonated the strongest with you? Select two or three. Give some explanation as to why you chose those miracles.

15. Which of the miracles do you think were most impactful on the disciples? Why?

16. Which of the miracles do you think were most impactful on the people who witnessed them? Why?

17. There are three invitations from Jesus that are remarkable in the book of John. Look up the following verses and explain why these invitations are remarkable.

    a. John 1:39
    b. John 7:37
    c. John 21:12

18. The quote below was used in the first lesson of this study of Jesus's miracles. In conclusion, reflect again on the quote and

share some of your observations and feelings about miracles and this study of the miracles of Jesus.

What is a miracle? Let me give you a simple definition. A miracle is an interference with nature by a supernatural power. A miracle is something outside our box invading our little box, something outside our world coming into our world and making waves and ripples. Miracles are events in the external world wrought by the power of God. A miracle is God stepping into the universe, setting aside the normal laws of nature to do a supernatural act. And therein you have the definition of miracles, really. They were mighty works to create wonder, to act as a sign.[84]

[84] MacArthur, "The Bible Verifiable by Miracles," https://www.gty.org/library/sermons-library/1346/the-bible-verifiable-by-miracles.

BIBLIOGRAPHY

"Miracles of Jesus." Accessed March 1, 2019. https://www.allaboutjesuschrist.org/miracles-of-jesus.htm.

"The First Sign: Jesus Turns Water Into Wine (John 2:1–11)." Accessed March 1, 2019. https://www.bible.org/seriespage/5-first-sign-jesus-turns-water-wine-john-21-11.

"Miracles." Accessed March 1, 2019.
https://www.biblegateway.com/resources/encyclopedia-of-the-bible/Miracles.

biblegateway.com. "Why Miracles?" Accessed March 1, 2019.
https://www.biblegateway.com/resources/ivp-nt/Why-miracles.

biblestudytools.com. "water." (italics added). https://www.biblestudytools.com/dictionary/water/.

blueletterbible.org. Mary Elizabeth Baxter. "Widow of Nain." Accessed March 1, 2019. https://www.blueletterbible.org/Comm/baxter_mary/WitW/WitW36_WidowOfNain.cfm.

blueletterbible.org. David Guzik. "Study Guide for Luke 8." https://www.blueletterbible.org/comm/guzik_david/study-guide/luke/luke-8.cfm.

blueletterbible.org. Clarence Larkin. "The Mystery of the Translation of the Living Saints." Accessed March 1, 2019. https://www.blueletterbible.org/study/larkin/dt/27.cfm.

christianquotes.info. "Miracles." Accessed March 1, 2019. https://www.christianquotes.info/search/miracles.

cgg.org. Martin G. Collins. "The Miracles of Jesus Part One, 3. What was the main purpose of Christ's miracles?" Accessed March 1, 2019. https://www.cgg.org/index.cfm/library/biblestudy/id/1173/miracles-jesus-christ.htm.

crosswalk.com. "In the Bible believers are with the Savior in eternity." Accessed March 1, 2019. https://www.crosswalk.com/faith/spiritual-life/this-too-shall-pass-is-in-the-bible-isnt-it.html.

desiringgod.org. "Four Truths About God's Provision." Accessed March 1, 2019. https://www.desiringgod.org/articles/four-truths-about-gods-provision.

desiringgod.org. "The Centurion: Faith that Made Jesus Marvel." Accessed March 1, 2019. https://www.desiringgod.org/articles/the-centurion-faith-that-made-jesus-marvel.

Elwell, Walter. "Miracles in the Old Testament." Edited by Walter Elwell. *Baker's Evangelical Dictionary of Biblical Theology.* Grand Rapids: Baker Book House Company, 1966.

faithweb.com. "The Mystery of the Divine Indwelling." Accessed March 1, 2019. Mysteries of The Bible Pt. 1 (faithweb.com).

faithweb.com. "The Mystery of the Incarnation." Accessed March 1, 2019. Mysteries of The Bible Pt. 1 (faithweb.com).

gileadfriendschurch.org. "Jesus Healed Peter's Mother-in-Law." Accessed March 1, 2019. https://www.gileadfriendschurch.org/jesus-healed-peters-mother-in-law.html.

gotquestions.org. "Are the miracles in the Bible to be taken literally?" Accessed March 1, 2019. https://www.gotquestions.org/miracles-literal.html.

gotquestions.org. "Is there activity of demonic spirits in the world today?" Accessed March 1, 2019. https://www.gotquestions.org/demonic-activity.html.

gotquestions.org. "What can we learn from Jesus' feeding of the 5000?" Accessed March 1, 2019. https://www.gotquestions.org/feeding-the-5000.html.

gotquestions.org. "What is the difference between miracles and magic?" Accessed March 1, 2019. https://www.gotquestions.org/difference-miracles-magic.html.

gotquestions.org. "What does it mean that the Bible is infallible?" Accessed March 1, 2019. https://www.gotquestions.org/Bible-infallible.html.

gotquestions.org. "What does the Bible mean by longsuffering?" Accessed March 1, 2019. https://www.gotquestions.org/Bible-longsuffering.html.

gotquestions.org. "What does the Bible say about thankfulness/gratitude?" Accessed March 1, 2019. https://www.gotquestions.org/Bible-thankfulness-gratitude.html.

gotquestions.org. "Who were the twelve (12) disciples/apostles of Jesus Christ?" Accessed March 1, 2019. https://www.gotquestions.org/twelve-apostles-disciples-12.html.

gotquestions.org. "Why did Jesus command people to not tell others of the miracles He performed?" Accessed March 1, 2019. https://www.gotquestions.org/do-not-tell.html.

gotquestions.org. "Why did Jesus allow the demons to enter the herd of pigs?" Accessed March 1, 2019. https://www.gotquestions.org/Jesus-demons-pigs.html.

Henry, Matthew. 2010. "Mark 5:21–34." *The New Matthew Henry Commentary*.1578. Grand Rapids: Zondervan, 2010.

Laidlaw, John. *The Miracles of Our Lord*. Grand Rapids: Zondervan, 1961.

learnreligions.com. Mary Fairchild. "Miracles of Jesus: From Healing the Sick to Turning Water Into Wine." Updated December 05, 2022. https://www.learnreligions.com/miracles-of-jesus-700158.

Ligonier.org. "Does R.C. Sproul Believe in Miracles?" Accessed March 1, 2019. https://www.ligonier.org/learn/articles/does-rcsproul-believe-miracles.

Ligonier.org. "Feeding Four Thousand." Accessed March 1, 2019. https://www.ligonier.org/learn/devotionals/feeding-four-thousand.

livingwordlightoflife.com. "Jesus Heals Peter's Mother-in-Law." Accessed March 1, 2019. https://www.livingwordlightoflife.com/jesus-heals-peters-mother-in-law.

Lockyer, Herbert. "The Miracle of the Nobleman's Son." *All the Miracles of the Bible*. Grand Rapids: Zondervan Publishing House, 1961. 160–251.

MacArthur, John. "The Bible Verifiable by Miracles." Accessed March 1, 2019. https://www.gty.org/library/sermons-library/1346/the-bible-verifiable-by-miracles.

Micklem, E.R. "Woman with a Haemorrhage." *Miracles and the New Psychology*. London: Oxford University Press, 1922.

Oxford Languages. "Miracle." Accessed March 1, 2019. miracle - Quick search results | Oxford English Dictionary (oed.com).

Ponder, Doug. "Why Did Jesus Turn Water Into Wine?" *Tabletalk Magazine*. December 2018. Ligonier Ministries.

Smith, William. *Smith's Bible Dictionary*. Nashville: Thomas Nelson, 1986. digital-Logos Research Edition, Logos release date 2001. https://www.logos.com.

Van Dixhoorn, Chad. *Confessing the Faith*. Edinburgh: Banner of Truth. 2014.

Walvoord, John F. and Roy B. Zuck. "The Healing of the Woman with a Hemorrhage." *The Bible Knowledge Commentary*. Wheaton: Victor Books, 1983.

Walvoord, John F. and Roy B Zuck. "Jesus Accused of Demonic Power." *The Bible Knowledge Commentary.* Wheaton: Victor Books, 1983.

Wiersbe, Warren. "Jesus the Host." *Bible Exposition Commentary.* Electronic Edition. Wheaton: Victor Books, a Division of Scripture Press Publications, Inc., 1996. https://www.logos.com.

Wiersbe, Warren. "John." *Bible Exposition Commentary.* Electronic Edition. Wheaton: Victor Books, a Division of Scripture Press Publications, Inc., 1996. https://www.logos.com.

Wiersbe, Warren. "Miracles in Mark." *Bible Exposition Commentary.* Electronic Edition. Wheaton: Victor Books, a Division of Scripture Press Publications, Inc., 1996. https://www.logos.com.

Wiersbe, Warren. "The Disciples." *Bible Exposition Commentary.* Electronic Edition. Wheaton: Victor Books, a Division of Scripture Press Publications, Inc., 1996. https://www.logos.com.

Wiersbe, Warren. "The Pharisees: False Piety." *Bible Exposition Commentary.* Electronic Edition. Wheaton: Victor Books, a Division of Scripture Press Publications, Inc., 1996. https://www.logos.com.

Wiersbe, Warren. "Victory Over Disease." *Bible Exposition Commentary.* Electronic Edition. Wheaton: Victor Books, a Division of Scripture Press Publications, Inc., 1996. https://www.logos.com.

Wiersbe, Warren. "We Are Fishers of Men—Obey Him." *Bible Exposition Commentary.* Electronic Edition. Wheaton: Victor Books, a Division of Scripture Press Publications, Inc., 1996. https://www.logos.com.

BONUS SECTION
Leading Others in Bible Study

Part 1 Introduction

People often ask me why I am interested in writing Bible studies and why I am interested in leading others in the Bible studies I write. Why is it that I am particularly interested in writing Bible studies? Why do I like to lead others in the studies I write? Why do I want to help you learn how to lead others in the study of God's Word? While the reasons may be many, there are three primary ones.

First, I know that I have been given a special love for writing. I have written extensively in my professional career in human resources, and I have written even more extensively in the creation of Bible studies for individuals and groups over the years. The Bible studies I am writing now are known as the Believers Bible Study Series (BBS), and I have been writing lessons for this study for more than twenty years.

Second, all Christians are given gifts from the Holy Spirit, and those gifts are to be used to serve God as much as a believer can. Since I believe one of my God-given gifts is to write lessons based on the Bible, I believe it is also it is my responsibility, joy, and honor to lead others in service to the Lord. There are many verses in the

Bible that point out why I should do these things, and two of the better-known ones are from Matthew 28:19–20 and 1 Peter 4:10,

> **God's Word Speaks**
> "Go therefore and make disciples of all nations, baptizing them in the name of the Father and of the Son and of the Holy Spirit, teaching them to observe all that I have commanded you." Matthew 28:19–20

> **God's Word Speaks**
> "As each has received a gift, use it to serve one another, as good stewards of God's varied grace." 1 Peter 4:10

Third, this is one of the areas of my life where I am truly driven to do work for the Lord and for other people. While I certainly get great joy from writing lessons and sharing stories about Jesus, I get even more joy when people I lead in study get as excited as I am about God's Word. Well-written lessons that are led with enthusiasm can and should lift the spirits of all who hear the Word when believers meet together in fellowship.

When I become lost in the Bible, the darkest day can turn bright, and the gloomiest day can become filled with joy. His Word is so powerful that one can handle all problems and issues because of the Bible's content. That's not to say the Bible will literally answer every question and solve every issue you have, but it does mean that somewhere in the Bible there are words that can make your day better.

However, my words should not be the ones that convince anyone of the value of knowing who God is and what His Word can do for those who believe. Consider the following two passages which demonstrate the power and purpose of the Word to lead us to understanding who God is and what His Word is intended to do.

God's Word Speaks

"For the word of God is living and active, sharper than any two-edged sword, piercing to the division of soul and of spirit, of joints and of marrow, discerning the thoughts and intentions of the heart." Hebrews 4:12

The Bible gets even more specific in what it can do as recorded in 2 Timothy.

God's Word Speaks

"All Scripture is breathed out by God and profitable for teaching, for reproof, for correction, and for training in righteousness, that the man of God may be complete, equipped for every good work." 2 Timothy 3:16–17

Part 2 Keys to an Effective Study: Planning and Steps

Anything we do has to have a plan of some sort even though that plan might be in your mind rather than on paper or on a computer. Getting started to lead a Bible study is no different. You will need to know some basic facts and ask some important questions before you begin. While the list below is not exhaustive, these are some of the keys to an effective study.

Beginning Steps: Questions to Ask and Answer

Why would you want to write and/or lead a Bible study?

Is it personal? Do you want to learn more about the Bible? Do you see a need for others to know about God's Word? Is it your great passion to help others know the grace of God, the love of Christ, and the power of the Holy Spirit?

How knowledgeable do you consider yourself when it comes to the Bible?

Do you feel confident that you can answer any (or most) questions asked in a lesson or might be asked by your group? If you don't, do you know where to find the answers? Are you willing to make yourself vulnerable by not being able to have the right answer or to answer any questions that might be asked? Are you willing to do the research after the fact to get an answer to questions that might be raised?

What is the level of Bible knowledge of those you want to lead in a study?

Will your audience's knowledge of the scriptures be basic, average, above average, or a mixture of all three? If you are creating the study yourself, this question is important because you will design and write questions of different levels of difficulty appropriate for the level of knowledge of the group. If using a prepared study, you will need to research the study to determine the difficulty level of the questions. As an example, for a less knowledgeable class, you will want to have basic questions while you can have questions with more depth for those who have been in Bible studies before. You may want to start with a simpler, shorter book such as "James" for those first starting to study, whereas you could lead a study based on a book written by Paul or one from the Old Testament if your class is more knowledgeable. With a mixed group, you will want to have some questions for all levels.

What will be the gender makeup of your study group?

Why is this important? There are some issues that will be gender-sensitive, and you need to make certain that the questions you ask are not offensive to one gender or the other.

Do you have the requisite skills to lead a class and manage the class interactions and time parameters once the class has begun?

How well do you deal with silence when no one wants to talk? How do you get people to talk? Can you handle conflict within a group? Are you able to control the pace of a group so that you cover all the material you planned to cover?

Do you want to lead a group based on the Bible alone, the Bible and a Christian book, or a Christian book alone?

The answer to this question may come down to how comfortable you are with the Bible as the primary proof text for your study. For purposes of what follows in these guidelines, the assumption is that the study is based on the Bible with support from commentaries and subject-matter experts who have authored books on your topic of choice. For example, John MacArthur, John Piper, and Tim Keller all provide scriptural background for their writings.

These are a few of the more important questions you need to answer before beginning a study group. There are more, and there will most likely be additional ones each time you get together. But for now, consider each one of the questions above to make sure you feel as comfortable as possible before you get started. Always keep in mind that what you do should be done for God's glory and to enhance the kingdom of God on earth. Once you are assured that God's path for you is to write and lead others, I promise that you will be more blessed than those you lead.

Prayer: The Most Important Step in Preparing to Study and Lead

If you are going to write the study to be used or if you are going to use a prepared study, go to the Lord in prayer before you begin. Pray that the Holy Spirit will be with you and will guide you in preparation or the choosing of a study. If you don't know what to pray or even how to pray depend on Romans 8:26.

> **God's Word Speaks**
> "Likewise, the Spirit helps us in our weakness. For we do not know what to pray for as we ought, but the Spirit himself intercedes for us with groanings too deep for words." Romans 8:26

Background Details: What You Need to Know When Studying the Bible

Once you have answered the questions about leading a study, and after you have prayed, you will need to pay attention to several important details about the book of the Bible or the portion of the scripture that will be the focus of what you are studying.

1. Understand when the book or passage was written. This will place it in the context of God's story and in man's history.
2. Know to whom the book or passage was written. A book or passage written to Jews will take a different slant than one written to Gentiles.
3. Identify the key people in the book or passage of the scripture you are studying. Find out what you can about each of those people.

Example: Hebrews is a great example of why the time, the people written to, and the people written about are important parts of what you need to know. The Hebrew people were Jews who were living after Jesus's ascension but before the destruction of the Jewish temple in Jerusalem in AD 70.

There were three groups of people the author of Hebrews focused on: (1) Jews who had accepted Christ as the Son of God and their Savior, (2) Jews who had intellectually accepted Christ but had not received Him as their Savior and Lord, and (3) Jews who chose to remain practicing Jews and rejected Christ as the Messiah. So to understand the letter and its purpose, you also need to understand these facets of what was going on in the hearts and minds of those to whom the letter was being written.

Part 3 The Inductive Bible Study Method

Part 2 of *Leading Others in Bible Study* focused on the planning and steps for beginning to lead others. Part 3 gives guidelines for one widely popular method of studying the Bible: *the inductive study method.* This is an investigative study method that provides an overall understanding of a passage of scripture. It starts with a passage and attempts to infer a principle or teaching. The opposite type of study is the deductive method which starts with some principle or teaching and attempts to find supporting passages.

For example, the inductive method used to study a parable of Jesus uses certain steps to get to the point of understanding what Jesus was teaching. You would read the parable and then determine what the guiding principle is intended to be. Whereas, with the deductive method, you would first determine the principle and then use the parable to demonstrate that principle.

You can read about the inductive study method and its efficacy from many sources. The information provided below is from *Logos Bible Software,* a software that I use extensively in Bible study preparation.

The inductive study is a very practical method as demonstrated by three precepts it embraces: (1) *observation* which leads to discovering what the passage says, (2) *interpretation* of what the passage means, and (3) *application* which shows a person how to apply what has been learned. While the first two precepts are important, the final one is what a study of scripture should do for all of us—show us how to apply God's Word to our lives.

To get to the three precepts listed above, the inductive study method offers some very specific steps to help you understand the part of scripture you might be studying. While these may not be exhaustive, they are certainly worth doing every time you begin to write a study and/or prepare to lead a study.

First, read the passage you have chosen and determine some basic and simple facts about the passage. Ask *who, what, when, where, why,* and *how.* When you answer these questions, you will be well on your way to understanding the passage of scripture. Multiple readings will help you put more in-depth definitions around the book, chapter, or passage you plan to use as the basis for the study.

Read the passage again in its entirety; find words or phrases throughout the passage that highlight a specific topic. Words or phrases such as these will help you understand what the author is trying to emphasize rather than you depending on yourself to make those decisions.

Next, look for repeated words or phrases. Why is this important? Any time a word or phrase is repeated is an indication that the word or phrase is most likely important to an overall meaning. As an example, the word *faith* is used over 400 times in the Bible. That gives you an idea of how important that concept is in the Bible as a whole.

Then make a list of concepts or ideas. When Jesus and the disciples were on a boat in the Sea of Galilee and a strong storm came about, you could see ideas such as the disciples' fear, the calm of Jesus, or the concern Jesus had that His disciples were not yet getting it as far as who He was.

There are many ways to study the Bible, and all of them when carried out with the guidance of the Holy Spirit will prove beneficial.

Part 4 Step-by-Step Recommendations

The Believers Bible Study Series provides a means of examining God's Word. The study has been around for over twenty years having started as an offshoot of working with young people in a youth ministry program. BBS is a group of men who meet weekly for approximately one and one-half hours to discuss God's Word and to grow in fellowship with one another. The study has been done both in person and more recently in a Zoom format. Remarkably, and because of what God does in the hearts of people through the Holy Spirit, both formats have proven to be successful.

The steps and recommendations that follow are those used by BBS in the weekly meeting. They are based on what has worked well for many years. As you begin to consider leading others, this method of study will enable you, if used generally in this format, to create an environment to study the Bible in a friendly, Christ-centered, Holy Spirit-led way for those desiring to better know and understand God and His Word. I know from personal experience that this study method will help you lead with excitement and joy!

Step 1
Pray. The group leader or someone in the group opens with a prayer for the evening. During prayer, concentrate on seeking the guidance of the Holy Spirit. Ask the Holy Spirit to lead the study so that the lessons that are learned will be those that are pleasing to the Lord. (Note: Before asking anyone to pray, check to make sure that the person selected does not mind praying in a public format.)

Step 2
Establish a method of calling on each person during the study time. If the study is in person, you might use the order in which

the individuals arrive or where they are seated around the room. If the study is on Zoom, you could use the order in which they sign on to the call or an alphabetical list of members or even a random selection. Whatever works best and is comfortable for you and the group is what is important.

Step 3
Using your established method of calling on each person, ask the first person on your list to read and respond to the first question. This step is valuable because it is the ideal way to get someone talking and to get as much participation as possible during the study. (Note: Make it clear that any member of the group can always pass when it is their turn.)

Step 4
After the first person has responded, ask if anyone else in the group has additional information they would like to share regarding the question. As the leader, you will need to make sure the group stays on point in the discussion, does not ramble on, or does not go off on rabbit trails as this will be a distraction and dilute the depth of the lesson. By controlling those who like to talk a lot or get off topic, you will also make sure to keep the group focused and on time in order to finish the study in the time allotted.

Step 5
Repeat Step 3 by asking the second person on your list to read and answer the next question. Continue doing this until all group members have had the opportunity to be the first to answer a question. When that has happened, return to the beginning of the list to continue the process until all the questions have been asked and answered.

Step 6
Once the lesson is completed, invite the members of the group to share prayer requests. Never force someone to provide a request, but you should also make sure that you give everyone the opportunity to share. It is important to tell the group that what is shared in the question answers and the prayer requests is confidential and is not to be shared with others outside the group. (Note: This provides a sense of safety in being open to sharing personal requests.) Make a list of the requests that are offered so that you can provide the group with a summary of the prayer requests.

Step 7
Close the study in prayer either by asking a class member to pray or taking a few minutes for each person to pray. How you do this will be based on the group's or your preference and time constraints.

Step 8
If meeting in person, hand out or assign the lesson at the end of the time together. If meeting on Zoom, send the lesson either later that same day or the next day after the study, send the next lesson to your group via email or some other means (never more than twenty-four hours after the close of the study.) It is a positive move to send the next lesson out on or about the same day and time each week. By doing it that way the group will be anticipating when they will receive the next study.

Whichever way the next lesson gets to the group members, follow-up communication is important. It is a good idea to include some key points from the completed study and the upcoming study along with the inclusion of the prayers that have been requested by the group.

Step 9
Close your email in which you send out the next lesson with a statement that is the same each week. This will create an idea that is consistent and that resonates with the group. As an example, a closing might be something such as "God loves you, and so do I!" or "Jesus cares for you!" This is strictly your choice; just keep it the same.

Step 10
Stay in touch with your group between the times you meet together. Ask them about the prayer requests they gave; if you find a good article on the Bible or an article on sharing God's Word, send it or just use the opportunity to say hi. Little connections mean a lot and build camaraderie and a sense of fellowship.

Part 5 Guidelines for Managing a Group

As the leader of the group, you are also the manager of what takes place throughout the time together. If this is not managed, the message may be hampered. To help the study stay as meaningful and as robust as possible, use the suggested guidelines listed below.

Guideline 1
Bible study should be fun since the Bible is all about the good news of Christ! We don't have senses of humor accidentally—God gives them to us just as He gives us all good things. This is not to say the study should be irreverent or insincere, but the study can be light-hearted and enjoyable without detracting from the power of God's Word.

Guideline 2

The steps outlined in the previous section should help minimize a lack of responses—or put positively, they should maximize responses you get by engaging everyone in the group. However, if it doesn't, don't let silence intimidate you. Wait a reasonable time; if no one has more to offer on a question, add a comment yourself or move on to the next question.

Guideline 3

You are the leader of the group, and for the most part, you should avoid sharing your answers too often. Make certain that you are not the first to respond to any question and that you share your answer to no more than two or three of the questions. When you do share, do so only after all or most of the group members have shared. Note that if something is said that is contradictory to Christian beliefs, you need to make that known as tactfully as possible.

Guideline 4

If your group has a question or questions that you don't have the answer to (and that will happen), let the group know you will research it and get back to them. And then be sure you follow through to find the answer. You can share the answer before the next class or at the beginning of the next class.

Guideline 5

Manage any rabbit trails that might come up. (See Step 4 in the previous section.)

Guideline 6

There will almost always be people in the group who like to pontificate. That may be someone who is excited about what they have to share, or it may be a person who has a need to be recognized for his knowledge (being needy). It is great to have people who are eager to share, but if they are allowed to dominate week after week, you will lose control. If it continues week after week, others in the group are likely to get frustrated and possibly shut down or even leave the study.

Managing the pontificator can be challenging because there are often people who communicate this way on a regular basis. One of the best ways to deal with them is to look for a break in their delivery. Tell them you really enjoy what they have to say, but you want to hear from some of the others in the group in order to keep things moving. It is also effective to regularly share with the entire group the necessity to keep answers as succinct as possible. This can easily be done when you communicate with the members by email or other means of correspondence. It is obvious that you should never mention a person by name when discussing this issue with the group.

In closing this guide to leading others, always keep in mind that Bible study—getting to know God the Father, God the Son, and God the Holy Spirit—is the most important thing you can do with your life. Your study, preparation, and leading time will be one of the most joyful times you spend as you immerse yourself and others in the Bible. You will be providing life lessons not just for the present but for eternity. There is no way you can serve mankind better than to help people know the Lord and what He can do in their lives!

Part 6 Frequently Asked Questions (FAQs)

Q. I'm not trained in the Bible. Why might I be qualified to lead others?

A. Leading others in Bible studies is more a heart issue than a head issue. If you love the Lord's Word and have a passion for it, with the Holy Spirit's help, you will be able to lead a study.

Q. How do I get started leading others in the study of the Bible?

A. One of the best places to start is by answering the questions in *Part 2 Keys to An Effective Study.* Once those questions are answered, you should have a good feeling as to whether this is what God is leading you to do. (Remember—always pray for guidance and entrust yourself to His plan.)

Q. How do I go about getting others to join me in a study?

A. Invite some people you know to meet with you to learn what God's Word is all about. These may be friends, fellow church members, or people from work. Don't ask too many to start with; ask a few that you really know and have a good feeling about. If this is what you are supposed to do, others will follow later.

Q. How can I determine who my target group members should be?

A. This will depend a lot on what your purpose for leading a study is. If you want other people to feel as excited about the Bible as you do, ask people who know or want to know the Bible. If you want to introduce the Bible to people, seek people new to church and worship from your church or people who have given an indication they want to know what the Bible is all about. You may want to focus on your own denomination or make it a cross-denomination study. And there certainly could be the possibility that you want to reach out to those who do not know Jesus.

Q. What is the best version of the Bible to use in a study?

A. The best version of the Bible to use is one with which you are most comfortable! There are two major types of versions available. One is known as thought for thought such as the *New International Version* (NIV); the other is word for word such as the *English Standard Version* (ESV), one of the best of this type. The first type deals more with the general thought of what the original was saying while the second type takes greater effort to translate words closer to the original languages of the Bible (Hebrew, Greek, and Aramaic). A Bible like *The Message* (MSG) is more like a commentary and is written in modern language but can be valuable to understanding difficult passages.

Q. Are there free online resources that will help me understand parts of scripture?

A. There are countless resources that are available. The biggest challenge is to find those that are factual and true to God's Holy Word in the original languages. Three of the very best are www.blueletterbible.org, www.biblehub.com, and www.gotquestions.org. All of these have great commentary on scripture. The first two have multiple commentaries and different versions of the

Bible. There is also help with understanding Greek and Hebrew words in the Blue Letter Bible.

Q. Are there online resources I can pay for that would be helpful?

A. Yes. One of the best is www.logos.com. There is a free basic version of the software, but with added features, there is a cost, and it can be expensive. A site that appraises Bible software, www.patheos.com, calls *Logos* the "Cadillac of Bible software." To find others—both free ones and ones that cost—just enter Bible software on the search line of your computer.

Q. Will the *Believers' Bible Study Series* offer further lessons that can be used in Bible studies I might want to study and/or lead?

A. *The Miracles of Jesus* is the first study to be published. Multiple studies have been written and used with the original group of men. The plan is for those studies to be published at a future date in a format similar to *The Miracles of Jesus.* The next one slated for possible publication is *The Parables of Jesus.*

Printed in the United States
by Baker & Taylor Publisher Services